The Story

of

YOU

The Story
of
YOU

**An Enneagram Journey
to Becoming Your True Self**

IAN MORGAN CRON

HarperOne
An Imprint of HarperCollinsPublishers

FIRST HARPERCOLLINS PAPERBACK PUBLISHED IN 2022

Designed by Nancy Singer

Library of Congress Cataloging-in-Publication Data is available upon request.

ISBN 978-0-06-282582-7

22 23 24 25 26 LSC 10 9 8 7 6 5 4 3 2 1

For Cail, Madeleine, and Aidan

Thank you for blessing my story.

Contents

The Stories We Tell

*Recognizing the Myth
of Who You Are*

"The universe is made of stories, not of atoms."
—Muriel Rukeyser

When I dragged myself into my first twelve-step meeting for people battling substance addiction, I felt more self-conscious than a bastard at a family reunion. Like most shame-riddled newcomers who fear rejection, I was sheepish about asking anyone to be my sponsor.

But there was this one guy.

Jack, a seventy-five-year-old retired Episcopal priest and therapist, was a recovery superhero. Whenever he spoke at meetings, his wry sense of humor and hard-won wisdom were apparent to everyone. He was a beacon of hope to those of us who had earned our seats in "the rooms." One night after a meeting, I mustered up the courage to introduce myself to him and ask if he'd consider taking me under his wing.

Jack's face softened, a smile appearing behind his eyes. "How long since you last drank or drugged?" he asked.

"Two weeks," I said, looking down at my shoes.

"Congratulations!" he said, throwing his arms around me and hugging me so enthusiastically I thought he might break one of my ribs. "I'll take you on!"

Under Jack's mentorship, my two weeks of sobriety stretched into one month, then two, and before I knew it, I received my anniversary chip marking three continuous months. My life was humming along swimmingly until Jack dropped a bomb on me at one of our weekly Sunday morning check-in meetings at the Colonial Diner.

"I signed you up to share your story at next week's Sunday night speaker's meeting," he said, stirring two packets of sugar into his coffee.

Recovery groups offer different meeting formats. In a speaker's meeting, one person shares their story—what their life was like before and while they were using, and the "experience, strength, and hope" they're finding through the program and working the steps. It's kind of like a personal testimony you might hear at a Baptist church, only boozier.

"Jack, you'd tell me if you'd had a stroke, right?" I said, only half-kidding.

"No, why do you ask?" Jack said, arching one eyebrow.

"Because I've only been sober for three months. I'm not ready!"

"You don't have to deliver the Gettysburg Address," he said, chuckling.

For the next thirty minutes I came up with one lame excuse after another to get out of speaking, but Jack wouldn't budge. Resigned to my fate, I stood up and lay down a five on the Formica-topped table.

"See you on Sunday," I muttered, picking up my windbreaker and walking to the door.

"Get yourself to five meetings this week," Jack called after me.

Without turning around, I waved goodbye. "Yeah, yeah, I know."

Over the next seven days, I wrote and trashed at least a dozen drafts of my life story. During my last pharmaceutical jag, I had suffered a series of panic attacks and was still terrified of losing control in public. But I slaved away until I had an acceptable draft of my chemical misadventures and rehearsed it, ignoring the movies in my head featuring projectile vomiting and images from Edvard Munch's "The Scream."

That Sunday night I stood before two hundred people and told the "story of me," at least as I understood it at the time. I described how I'd always felt like a "troubled guest on the dark earth."[1] I was sure I lacked something inside that everyone else seemed to have—I felt like a college freshman who'd missed orientation week and didn't know his way around campus like everyone else. I enumerated the long list of reasons for my tattered self-worth, including my father's death from alcoholism and how I'd still give anything to believe I wasn't somehow responsible for his inability to love me. Then I described how I felt when I took my first drink—finally, at home in my own skin, fitting in, at ease in the world. Except that back then my life was sort of like *The Glass Castle* meets *The Prince of Tides*—only less hopeful.

But when the meeting ended, I felt like a celebrity. Person after person came up to tell me the parts of my story they identified with and to thank me for my willingness to share it. When the last one left, I helped fold and stack the chairs, wash the coffee urns, and left with Jack riding shotgun in my Toyota Corolla.

"You did a good job tonight," he said, rolling down the passenger-side window to release the smoke from his signature Cuban cigar.

"Thanks," I said, relieved to be over my first attempt at sharing my life's journey.

"It's interesting," Jack mused. "While you were speaking, I found myself thinking about the crazy story each of us comes up with to make sense of our lives." He gazed at the smoke wafting up and out the car window, seemingly lost in his own thought.

When I pulled up at the end of Jack's driveway, he offered his congratulations one last time and got out of the car, hobbling on his creaky knees. I was about to put the car in drive and pull away when he turned back around.

"One more thing," he said, bending over to speak to me through the open passenger window. "Do you ever wonder if you're living in the wrong story?"

"Uh, no," I said, trying not to frown.

"You might," Jack said, double-tapping the roof of my car with his hand. Then he turned on his heels and began trudging up the driveway, disappearing into the night's inky darkness.

The Power of the Enneagram

I was twenty-seven years old when Jack asked me that question. At the time, I dismissed it as the kind of oddball question only a septuagenarian therapist might pose when he's stayed up past his bedtime.

Today, I see Jack's question to me as a major turning point in changing the false story I told myself about who I was, a story that had helped me make sense of a painful childhood but became an obstacle to my growth as an adult.

My old story is captured in a snapshot I still have of me back when I was a little boy at the beach with my family. In the picture I'm sitting in a beached lifeguard boat waving and laughing at the camera. I remember it was a beautiful, sunny day. I'm squinting at the camera and everyone in the background is sporting Ray-Bans, baking in the sun, their bronze skin glistening with Hawaiian Tropic Dark Tanning Oil. It strikes me as ironic that I'm sitting in a lifeboat. My family was lost at sea in those days and though I was a child I remember sensing that my siblings and I were living under a low ceiling of gray clouds. Our troubled father was taking our ship down.

Fifteen years later, I was a hard-drinking partier being chased down by my friends in Young Life who viewed me as a prized evangelism project. But I wanted nothing to do with God. In childhood I'd loved him with all my heart, but I grew to believe that he'd abandoned me to my crazy family. Stretched out in front of me was a lifetime of feeling ashamed, weighted down with a longing to be seen and loved that I feared would never be fulfilled.

When I began working on my issues in my twenties, the green shoots of a new story began to emerge from the soil. It took years of hard work and prayer to craft a new narrative, but today when I look in the mirror, I see a sober husband and father, an Episcopal priest, therapist, and author.

Where there was old me, now there's a new me.

Where there was fear and shame, now there's dignity.

Where there was an unnamable missing piece everyone else had but I didn't, now there's the certain belief that I'm not missing anything inside.

Where there was loneliness and abandonment, I now have a kind and encouraging community that affirms my gifts.

Where there was grim resignation, now there's a serene acceptance that life is simultaneously hard *and* brimming with beauty and grace.

And where there was meaninglessness, now there's the knowledge that I continue to take everything I've experienced and use it to advance God's love into our riven world.

When I reached another major turning point in my life in discovering the Enneagram, it helped make sense of this dramatic before-and-after difference in my life. Even more important—and this is key to this entire book—it helped me learn what was fueling and sustaining my old story, and what I needed to do that would make it possible for me to keep moving into my new story. The transformation itself was all grace, but I had a choice either to resist or to receive it. I wish I'd known the Enneagram when I began the journey of writing a new story for myself. It would have saved me time.

Traditionally, the Enneagram refers to a personality typing system that helps people cultivate self-knowledge. (To learn more about the Enneagram, and to take a test to determine your Enneagram type, visit my website, ianmorgancron.com.) I'm an Enneagram Four, which is just one of the nine basic types of the system (*ennea* is the Greek root for the word nine). Called the Romantics, Fours are creative, imaginative people who are sensitive, empathic, and attuned to beauty and aesthetics. Sounds good, right? But, like all Enneagram types, they have a shadow side. In the Fours' case, it includes moodiness, a fear of abandonment, and the belief that they're irredeemably deficient, among other things.

Through the years I've learned that the Enneagram is a remarkably helpful tool for understanding myself and others. When I was first introduced to it during a difficult season in my life, its ability to describe my way of moving through the world amazed me. I became a devoted student of this ancient, uncannily accurate system of personality.

As my fascination and appreciation grew, I wrote a book about it, *The Road Back to You* (with Suzanne Stabile), and started a podcast (*Typology*) on which I explore the mystery of the human personality through the lens of the Enneagram.[2] In the pages ahead you'll meet my friends who were willing to show up and share their stories.

Several years into my study of the Enneagram, I had an *aha* moment that boosted my appreciation of its wisdom even more. Not only does its description of nine different types accurately describe our personality, but the Enneagram *reveals* the nine broken stories that each type adopts and inhabits in childhood to make sense of the world—destructive stories we continue to tell ourselves in adulthood about who we are and how the world operates.

As you'll learn, the self-defining stories we invent in childhood later wreak havoc on our lives, psychologically and spiritually, because the underlying premise of each is in direct opposition to the grace-filled Larger Story God wants us to enter into and enjoy.

The Enneagram also shows us how to escape our type's broken story by getting off the treadmill repetitions of self-defeating behaviors and misperceptions that often leave us frustrated, confused, and heartbroken.

What separates the Enneagram from other personality typing systems is that it helps us craft and live a better, truer story than the one we've unconsciously settled for. I'm going to tell you a bit later in the book how I've learned to do this myself.

Our Origin Story

Human beings are incurable storytellers. We tell hard luck stories, tall stories, short stories, cock-and-bull stories, sob stories, rags-to-riches stories, shaggy-dog stories, fish stories, one-sided stories, and the occasional "long story short."

What accounts for the power and everywhere-ness of stories? Our very survival depends on them. From the time we enter this world, we begin crafting a story that helps us make sense and give meaning to the painful things that happen to us.

Don't underestimate little kids. They're wicked smart. They don't just pick up messages from their family members and peers about who they are and what the world expects of them; they suck them up like Shop-Vacs. Over time, they naturally create an elaborate story about their identity and value based on these experiences and unconscious messages, a narrative that grooves itself deeply into their hearts.

This is the story that helped us, as children, know who we needed to be and what we needed to do to feel safe in the world. According to many therapists, we actually build our lives around this self-told story. It forms our identity and personality.

For example, if your father lavished you with praise only when you won in sports or if you heard the disappointment in your mother's voice when you got a B+ on your report card, did you think to yourself, "Oh well, my parents mean well but they're just shallow people who need me to be their little wunderkind to buoy their self-esteem and make them look good in the eyes of their friends at the country club"? Heck no, you likely noted their reactions and concocted a story around the message, "I have to win every game. I have to ace every test. I have to succeed at everything in life or people won't love me."

Or maybe you were a quiet and shy kid whose desires got swallowed up by outgoing friends and domineering siblings. Did you decide, "Hey, I'll get a big-ass bullhorn and force them to notice me"? Or did you unconsciously craft a story around the message, "No one ever hears or values my opinions or desires. Why waste time and energy voicing them?"

Maybe you endured the trauma of your parents' divorce, the sudden loss of a sibling, or the unpredictable behavior of an alcoholic family member. Could you see beyond the pain to conclude, "Life is full of beauty and terror, but in the end all shall be well"? Not a prayer. Even the poet Rilke couldn't come up with an insight like that at age seven. Instead, you probably reached a different conclusion more along the lines of, "The world is a scary, unpredictable, painful place. If I don't remain vigilant all the time, I won't be ready when disaster strikes again."

Now, notice how each of these life narratives runs contrary to the story of grace. Does God require us to succeed in order to be loved? Does God insist that we run ourselves into the ground with exhaustion before we can know peace? Does God say we will feel safe in the world only if we live in perpetual fear of the worst? I think not.

But once we tether ourselves to these stories it never occurs to us that we can interrogate or rewrite them. Every day becomes our very own personalized *Groundhog Day*. Like Bill Murray's film character trapped in a seemingly endless loop of repetition, we recycle the same events and mistakes again and again. We see what we've conditioned ourselves to see, no matter how much older we are or how different circumstances may be from the training ground of our childhood.

But here's the thing: these stories are worn-out myths. They're useful and necessary myths in childhood, for sure. But they make a mess of our lives when we continue to believe them uncritically in adulthood. As Carl Jung once wrote, "We cannot live the afternoon of life according to the programme of life's morning; for what was great in the morning will be little at evening, and what in the morning was true, will at evening have become a lie."[3] What supports us in childhood thwarts us in adulthood. Our old stories continue to operate autonomously in the shadows of the heart and become the enemy of our growth.

Fortunately, we can craft a different story in adulthood. We can't change the facts of what happened to us in the past, but we can change how we show up for life in the present. In the chapters ahead we'll learn how each of us can rewrite the survival story of our Enneagram type.

It's time to jettison the old story line. Doing so is within your power, and I wrote this book to show you how. As Mo Willems, the children's author, once wrote, "If you ever find yourself in the wrong story, leave."[4]

2

Changing Your Story

The Genius of the Enneagram

*"It's like everyone tells a story about themselves
inside their own head. Always. All the
time. That story makes you what you are.
We build ourselves out of that story."*
—Patrick Rothfuss

My friend Donald Miller understands the power of story. He's written a fair number of books, including several that help companies discover what their brand's story is and how to communicate it to customers.

To Don, the elements of a good story aren't complicated, whether it's for companies or individual people.[1] The problem is that so many people vaguely feel like they're living a story that no longer works for them. At one point earlier in his life, Don felt that way himself. He was struggling financially and says he "spent countless hours" feeling sorry for himself.[2] He also weighed 387 pounds, which is hard to reconcile with the healthy Don I know.

Normally, when you ask people who have lost a lot of weight how they did it, they'll rattle on about their ex-Navy SEAL gym trainer, or the industrial drums of carrot beet juice they drank every day, and you'll probably be sorry you ever asked. But Don didn't do that. When he explained to me how he had lost nearly half his body weight, he focused on something else entirely.

"How I got through that and changed was entering into a story that required me to weigh less," he said.

He entered into a new story. What a curious idea.

Along the way, he also dieted and rode his bike from Los Angeles to Delaware, so don't imagine his weight loss didn't require a ton of effort. (Sorry, folks.) But the key force driving him to do it was a determination to inhabit a different story than the one he'd been telling himself for most of his life.

"I think most people don't actually realize they have agency to write their story," he said.

Most of us are reading off old scripts, parts of which we wrote and parts of which have been handed down to us by the important people in our lives. In many cases, those scripts helped us navigate the rocky terrain of childhood and early adulthood. But, at some point, the stories stopped serving us and we started serving the stories. This is how we mortgage our futures.

Some of us have become vaguely aware that we've outgrown our old stories, but we don't know how to break out of them. Some of us are even less self-aware, mindlessly engaging in recurring cycles of the same old same old, wondering how we got into this mess—

again. As James Hollis says, "No one awakens in the morning, looks in the mirror, and says, 'I think I will repeat my mistakes today,' or 'I expect that today I will do something really stupid, repetitive, regressive, and against my best interests.' But, frequently, this repetition of history is precisely what we do, because we are unaware of the silent presence of those programmed energies, the core ideas we have acquired, internalized, and surrendered to."[3]

Here's what Don Miller said: "If you want to change, pick a new story." Could it really be that simple?

Your Old Story Isn't Working

Personal organizer Marie Kondo published a bestselling book a few years ago called *The Life-Changing Magic of Tidying Up*. If you haven't read it, the basic premise is that your whole life will improve when you start purging your stuff. (She lost me when she said you should only keep thirty books. But I digress.) The book's overall message was good: she told readers to take an inventory of each thing they were holding onto and ask themselves if it still "sparked joy." If it didn't, they were to say thank you to the object for any happiness or usefulness it once provided and then toss it into the donate pile.

Although that approach has some limitations (I'd rather eat glass than throw out my library), it's a useful springboard for what we can do with our old stories. Not to put too fine a point on it, but many of the stories we tell ourselves suck. They aren't useful or making us happy anymore. Instead, they're often making us (and others) miserable. We owe it to ourselves and to those we love to run for the exits.

Yes, we can say thank you to these stories before we say good-bye to them. They gave us a way to ascribe meaning to experiences, to form a coherent sense of self, and to create a suite of coping strategies. But changing them is not simply a matter of saying, "Thank you, bogus story, for all the ways you helped me in the past" and then tossing it into the donate pile because it's outlived its usefulness. Some stories are so ingrained we're slow to recognize they jumped the shark a long time ago.

Signs You're Living in a Broken Story

If we refuse our soul's summons to change our childhood narrative, we end up stuck. We want to change, but we don't know how.

At a very basic level, there's a powerful reason why it's difficult to recognize that these old childhood stories are running the show: *they're always there*. As the old saying goes, no prison is more secure than the one we don't know we're in.

Do you want to know if you might be living in an old, broken narrative? Consider these clues.

- You look in the rearview mirror of your life and see a debris field of broken relationships.
- You keep landing in the wrong job.
- You tend to stay in relationships far beyond their expiration date.
- You're physically, emotionally, and spiritually burned out and don't know why.
- You get angry in ways that seem disproportionate to the crimes.
- You react impulsively to people and circumstances instead of responding mindfully to them.

- You have a nagging suspicion you're reading off a script someone else handed you.
- You can't stop the constant negative self-commentary streaming through your mind.
- You've developed addictions that you know are masking pain you don't want to confront.
- You feel disappointed that your life has turned out to be smaller than you dreamed it would be.

You might already be aware of living in a broken story, and maybe even tried to change it. You've read books and gone on retreats, attended conferences and hired coaches and counselors, joined recovery groups and gotten sponsors. But even when you know the messages you internalized as a child aren't working for you as an adult, it takes more than Pilates or walking on hot coals at a Tony Robbins seminar to overcome them.

We're all fiercely loyal to our broken narratives—because who would we be without them?

Inside the Enneagram

The Enneagram gives us clues to who we are, both trapped in our false stories and freed to rewrite them. It presents a remarkable constellation of nine archetypal stories, common to all human experience, which we adopt and inhabit in childhood to make sense of who we are and to figure out how this strange new world works.

If you're thinking, *Only nine stories for the estimated 108 billion people who have ever lived on this planet? Preposterous!* I get it, but why not? Literary critics believe there are only seven basic plots in literature and film. Are these the *only* narratives that entrap us? I have no idea. All I know is these nine narratives appear so often among the human family that we should at least pay attention to them.

I'm going to introduce you to a number of wise people who have been using the Enneagram to recognize the broken story they bought into as kids, identify the ways it was limiting their lives, and live into the true story they can be writing instead. Here's an overview of how each of the nine types subscribes to a particular story.

TYPE EIGHT: The Challenger

The Eight's story centers around their belief that we live in a dog-eat-dog universe where the powerful dominate and take advantage of the innocent and weak. Intimidating, energetic, autocratic, self-confident, and commandeering, Eights assert strength and power over people and the environment to mask vulnerability and weakness from themselves and others. (It may seem strange to you that this list starts with type Eight instead of type One, but that's because of the structure of the Enneagram. Eights, Nines, and Ones are in the same "gut triad," so they appear together here and in the order of the chapters.)

TYPE NINE: The Peacemaker

The Peacemaker's story centers around the unconscious belief that the world thinks their presence doesn't matter. Therefore, to avoid disconnection and keep the peace, Nines believe they must go with the flow, avoid conflict, and merge with the preferences, viewpoints, and priorities of others. Easygoing, affable, and sometimes complacent, Nines don't assert themselves and risk becoming "self-less."

TYPE ONE: The Improver

Ones are honest, conscientious, detail-oriented, self-disciplined, and morally heroic people. The underlying false premise of their story is the belief that the world loves and rewards only the "good" people and judges the "bad" ones. If you're trapped in the Improver's story, you try to gain love and a sense of control by tamping down your anger, meeting your own high internal standards, and seeking to perfect yourself, others, and the world. (In *The Road Back to You*, this type was called the Perfectionist, but I've since moved to calling it the Improver. If I had a nickel for every One who thanked me for making this change, I'd be richer than Jeff Bezos.)

TYPE TWO: The Helper

Twos are giving, supportive, caring, and servant-hearted people who desperately want to be liked and appreciated. People inhabiting the hapless fiction of the Helper unconsciously believe they can't be loved for who they are, but only for what they do for others. It makes sense, then, that disavowing their own needs and helping others becomes their strategy for gaining love and approval.

TYPE THREE: The Performer

Threes are driven, goal-crushing, image-conscious, and accomplishment-focused people whose dominant story is based on the mistaken notion that being successful and avoiding failure at all costs is the only pathway to being valued and loved.

TYPE FOUR: The Romantic

Fours are creative, sensitive, temperamental, and emotionally intense people whose story revolves around the misguided idea that they're missing something crucial inside and until they regain it they will never be loved and understood or feel whole and welcome in the world. Addicted to their own suffering, they seek to shore up their shaky self-image and achieve belonging by appearing special and unique.

TYPE FIVE: The Investigator

Private, highly observant, analytical, and emotionally distant, the Five's story centers around the idea that the world is intrusive and makes more demands on them than they can meet. Thus, Fives protect themselves against intrusion by reducing their own needs, observing rather than participating in life, isolating, and gaining knowledge to fend off feelings of ineptitude and inadequacy.

TYPE SIX: The Loyalist

Warm, trustworthy, questioning, and anxious, the Loyalist's story revolves around their belief that the world is a dangerous place in which the only way to feel safe and certain is to remain hypervigilant, forge strong alliances, and prepare for the worst.

TYPE SEVEN: The Enthusiast

The self-limiting narrative of the Seven arises from their unconscious belief that painful emotions, thoughts, or situations must be avoided at all costs. Charming, intelligent, entertaining, future-focused, optimistic, and adventurous, Sevens are afraid of being trapped in negative feelings from which they can't escape.

Choosing a New Story

Enneagram fans will often express amazement at how well it describes them. But is that all it has to offer—a static description of our personality type that we can chat about at cocktail parties or post brainless memes about on Instagram? Heck, no. The Enneagram is a prescription for deep change.

The more I read about the Romantic's story (Four) the more I realized I'd been clinging to a narrative built on a lie. It distorted my self-understanding and prevented me from becoming who I truly am. If I wanted to become the healthiest, highest expression of Ian Cron I would have to exit the old story of the Romantic and enter into the Romantic's new one.

Listen: the sum of what I've learned as a psychotherapist, Episcopal priest, spiritual director, and as a person on my own journey of transformation boils down to one simple fact.

All transformation begins with story transformation.

You won't change if you don't break free from your old, self-defining childhood story. This is the work we have to do, and the Enneagram can help us. I could say a closing prayer and pass the collection basket right now, but there's much, much more for us to learn about re-authoring our stories.

Teacher Cynthia Bourgeault tells a brilliant parable in her book *The Wisdom Way of Knowing* that illustrates the battle we face to rid ourselves of our old story in order for a truer, better story to materialize:

Once upon a time, in a not-so-far-away land, there was a kingdom of acorns, nestled at the foot of a grand old oak tree. Since the citizens of this kingdom were modern, fully Westernized acorns, they went about their business with purposeful energy; and since they were midlife, baby-boomer acorns, they engaged in a lot of self-help courses. There were seminars called "Getting All You Can out of Your Shell." There were woundedness and recovery groups for acorns who had been bruised in their original fall from the tree. There were spas for oiling and polishing those shells and various acornopathic therapies to enhance longevity and well-being.

One day in the midst of this kingdom there suddenly appeared a knotty little stranger, apparently dropped "out of the blue" by a passing bird. He was capless and dirty, making an immediate negative impression on his fellow acorns. And crouched beneath the oak tree, he stammered out a wild tale. Pointing upward at the tree, he said, "We . . . are . . . that!"

Delusional thinking, obviously, the other acorns concluded, but one of them continued to engage him in conversation: "So tell us, how would we become that tree?"

"Well," he said, pointing downward, "it has something to do with going into the ground . . . and cracking open the shell."

"Insane," they responded. "Totally morbid! Why, then we wouldn't be acorns anymore."[4]

As long as your old shell remains in place, you will never become who you were intended to be—an oak tree. Your old story has to crack open so the seed of your authentic self can grow. I'm not saying that you're going to entirely change those unique traits that make you *you*. If you're an Investigator (Five), you're probably still going to value time alone and hungrily learning new things over engaging in small talk at crowded parties. But if you're ready to do the hard work, you'll discover the value and satisfaction that comes from cultivating deep, transparent relationships.

And if you're a Challenger (Eight), you can expose your tender heart and survive to tell the tale, learning that your own human weakness is, paradoxically, a strength.

This is difficult work. Entering a new and truer story won't occur without confronting the same resistance put up by the blind acorns in Bourgeault's parable.

Moving from Passion to Virtue

People often ask me, "What exactly do you mean when you say we have to do the work?" The work begins with recognizing and deconstructing our old story to make room for a better one. Then we start to deal with our type's Passion.

Fortunately, the Enneagram offers a map for getting from Point A (old and broken story) to Point B (new and better story). Everything we do together in this book is designed to help you move from your type's default Passion (your Point A) to its Virtue (your Point B), thereby rewriting your old story.

The words "Passion" and "Virtue" may sound confusing to you. (As Inigo Montoya put it in *The Princess Bride*, "You keep using that word. I do not think it means what you think it means.") In Enneagram-speak, your Passion is sometimes also referred to as a "deadly sin," which gives you a clue that it's about more than just a deep emotion. An Enneagram Passion isn't something you feel "passionate" about; it's a destructive influence, as in "consumed by passion" or a "crime of passion."

Your Passion is the ever-present, unconscious emotional force or motivation driving the self-defeating behaviors that, despite your best efforts, you haven't been able to stop. When you're in its grip, it causes you to act in ways that hurt yourself and others. It is the "lie" of your type, perpetuating the old, weary story as a doomed strategy for satisfying your needs and desires, like love, safety, or a sense of control. Ironically, it prevents you from realizing them.

Consider how this insight might be at work in your life: *Your Passion is the source of your suffering.* Its false promise is the enemy of your growth. If you don't believe that your Passion is the root of your pain, remember that the very word "Passion" comes from the Latin root for suffering, as in Christ's Passion and death.[5] It is the wellspring of the anguish you feel.

The Enneagram's built-in escape route is the corresponding Virtue of each type, which can overcome its Passion and dismantle its false story. In a simplified version of Enneagram teacher Oscar Ichazo's formulation, what we're calling "Point A" and "Point B" looks like this:[6]

	Passion	Virtue
The Challenger: Eight	Lust	Innocence
The Peacemaker: Nine	Sloth	Right Action
The Improver: One	Anger	Serenity
The Helper: Two	Pride	Humility
The Performer: Three	Deceit	Authenticity
The Romantic: Four	Envy	Equanimity
The Investigator: Five	Avarice	Nonattachment
The Loyalist: Six	Fear	Courage
The Enthusiast: Seven	Gluttony	Sobriety

Your path to liberation charted in the Enneagram starts with recognizing the ways your life has been limited by your type's Passion—and, through your Virtue, recognizing who you truly are when your Passion is no longer unconsciously running the show.

For instance, to counter their Passion, healthy Eights strive to recapture their innocence, revealing—and reveling in—the tender feelings they've taught themselves to bury deep down. One Eight I know, Chris Cruz, reconnects with his innocence when he's reading stories with his son. It's one of the rare times when he allows himself to feel vulnerable—which he says makes him feel "incredibly awkward, almost naked"—but it's a path forward in the new story he is authoring for himself, a story in which he has the courage to be defenseless.[7]

Improver Ones can cultivate serenity by accepting things as they are, not as they wish. The "serenity prayer" could have been written with a One in mind: "God, give me the serenity to accept the things I cannot change, the courage to change the things I can, and the wisdom to know the difference." Ones who realize they're not responsible for improving everything around them, who can learn "the wisdom to know the difference" between what is and isn't theirs to change, can acknowledge their inherent goodness and experience serenity. In serenity they stop labeling everything as good or bad or right or wrong and can release themselves of the exhausting need to fix everything. They can also be free of the equally exhausting need to excel at everything.

My friend Julianne Cusick, who is a One, says that when she was younger, her drive for perfection was often so crippling that she wouldn't try new things in case she proved to be bad at them.[8] This attitude kept her frozen in place for years, afraid to fail. Julianne says her new story has required her to learn the beautiful truth: that "anything worth doing is worth doing poorly. Let's just do it. Let's experience it, versus being crippled by fear of failure." Her new story could be called *Progress, Not Perfection*. When Improvers can say these words with conviction, they're well on the way to entering a new story.

SOAR

But of course, transformation is not simply a matter of learning, "Well, Improver, clearly your problem is that your old story involves a lot of being angry at the world and at yourself for not being perfect. Relax! Accept life on life's terms! C'est fini!"

Rather, it is a lifelong process of making choices that will lead to growth.

The genius of the Enneagram is that not only does it reveal *what* needs to change, but also *how* to change. Undertaking the journey of moving from Passion to Virtue has revolutionized my life, as it has the lives of the many individuals whose stories you'll hear in this book. You'll notice that four main elements are common to these Enneagram stories of transformation, which I describe as four steps to change under the rubric SOAR: See, Own, Awaken, and Rewrite.

See. Author Wendell Berry once wrote, "If you don't know where you're from, you'll have a hard time saying where you're going." The first step of transformation with the Enneagram is to see where your old story began—to exhume the hurtful events; the unchallenged, taken-for-granted beliefs; and the unhelpful internalized messages from your childhood that still rule your life today. I call this your origin story.

As a Four, I discovered that "seeing" meant diving into the story of what happened to me when growing up in a home with an alcoholic, drug-addicted father. It involved writing it down and sharing it with a trusted friend.

Don't panic if you don't consider yourself a writer. This will be a liberating exercise even if you're not John Irving. The "See" step will help you uncover all the false, self-limiting stories and mistaken beliefs about what you have to do and who you have to be in order to find love, safety, and a sense of control in a frightening world.

Own. The second step involves exploring both the shadow sides as well as the strengths of each type. This is an uncomfortable but healing exercise, and the more committed you are to it, the more you'll get out of it. No amount of Enneagram information can transform you unless you're rigorously honest with yourself about who you are. This requires an inventory, which is not an exercise in beating yourself up. Think of yourself as a store owner who is dispassionately taking stock of all the items in your shop. You look around and say, "Here's a curdled quart of milk that needs pitching. Here's a worm-infested tomato unworthy of throwing." You're discarding the old to make shelf space for the new.

For me, taking inventory helped me understand how the false beliefs and unconscious choices I made when I was trapped in my old story had damaged my self-worth and relationships. In the "Own" step I had to grieve the missed opportunities, how I had gotten derailed, and how I had taken comfort in drugs and drink in order to soothe my pain. But I also had to learn how to own what was most beautiful about me. It revealed my original goodness, that I was worthy of relationship and belonged in the world.

Awaken. As we recognize the effects of our old story in the past, we can move into the present. Our old stories have a trance-like quality. Once we've begun to see and own them, we can start waking up to how certain situations and stresses can trigger us to fall back into the old narrative.

A key part of this step is cultivating mindfulness, an important practice with the Enneagram. Without it, we can't self-observe our behaviors in real time. Mindfulness involves paying attention to what's happening in the present moment as we catch ourselves in the act of falling into our old story. The Enneagram teaches that, when we can stand back and "catch ourselves in the act," the grip of our Passion begins to dissolve. In the "Awaken" step, we develop increased awareness and learn how to resist the old gravitational pull of our Passion.

Rewrite. Addressing past and present readies us for making choices in light of the future. But how do we know what a transformed future will look like? Although it might sound passive, by this point you have cleared away so much debris that your new story will begin revealing itself without your having to force it.

However, there are also a couple of proactive things I'd suggest you do. The first is simply renaming your story. My old story used to be called *The Lost Boy.* Now I've titled it *The Redeemed Man.* In the rewrite, I am no longer the victim of my story; I am the hero. As you rename your story, you will be empowered to take the steps that help you live up to that new title.

Another proactive strategy lies in recognizing that re-authoring your narrative is a not a matter of one-and-done. It is the task of a lifetime. As you move away (oh yes, you will) from your type's default Passion and closer to its Virtue, you learn the power of doing the opposite of what you would normally do, responding to difficult situations (and people) in new and creative ways.[9] The goal is to challenge the old taken-for-granted beliefs of your false narrative to help you get unstuck.

There's an ancient spiritual practice that I include as part of the rewrite step—*agere contra*, literally "acting against." The concept comes from Saint Ignatius of Loyola. Father Edmund Lo, a Canadian Jesuit priest, says it's about actively rejecting old patterns that are keeping us stuck:

> We can be attached to patterns of behaviour that seemingly make us feel safer, be they our insecurities, doubts, or un-

willingness to be pulled out of our comfort zones. They prevent us from living our lives fully in the way the Lord intends. When we live our lives in Spirit and in Truth, we live in a true freedom. Agere contra helps us to confront those things that hold us back from such freedom; better yet, it helps us to grow into this freedom.[10]

Agere contra rests on the idea that we can, as Lo puts it, name whatever is owning us and driving our behavior—our old story. Then we can actively choose to do something else instead.

Agere contra is an important tool for this fourth step of SOAR. As you rewrite your narrative, ask yourself: *Who was I before the world told me who I was supposed to be? Who would I be and what could I achieve if I pushed back against the false story about who I think am and the nature of the world? What decisions can I make to-day to inhabit the new story that will help me become the highest and truest expression of myself?*

In the chapters ahead (as well as in the companion work-book you can do on your own or with a group), we'll explore the characteristic traits of each Enneagram type's survival story, then offer practical suggestions for growth in working through these four steps.

Now finally, and most importantly, before you begin "the work," remember that you were given something beautiful when you were given you. Something wants to be born into the world through your life. On my office wall I have a prayer written by George Appleton that I like to say from time to time. Perhaps it will help you as you embark on this journey of entering into a new story.

Give me a candle of the spirit, O God, as I go down into the
deep of my own being.
Show me the hidden things. Take me down to the spring of my
life, and tell me my nature and my name.
Give me freedom to grow so that I may become my true self—
the fulfillment of the seed which you planted in me at my
making.[11]

Now, let's get to it.

3

The Eight's Story

A Revolution for the Challenger

"There is a stubbornness about me that never can bear to be frightened at the will of others. My courage always rises with every attempt to intimidate me."
—Jane Austen, *Pride and Prejudice*

My ninety-three-year-old mother lives in an assisted living facility in Pennsylvania. At the start of the pandemic, I phoned her to find out if she felt anxious about catching the deadly virus that was tragically spreading like wildfire through continuing-care communities across the country.

"Has COVID attacked you yet?" I asked, knowing my mother would bristle if I approached the subject with that syrupy voice therapists use when they're trying too hard to sound empathic.

"It wouldn't dare," she said in her trademark husky voice.

Readers of *The Road Back to You* know that my Enneagram Eight mother smoked Pall Malls for seventy-five years. The only reason she finally kicked the habit was because her geriatrician warned her that her oxygen tank would detonate if she lit a match near it, and I was finally able to convince her that blowing herself up in the bingo hall would prove to be an uncomfortable experience for her.

"What makes you think you're immune to catching COVID?" I responded, stifling a laugh.

"My white blood cells would kick its butt," she roared in laughter.

My mom's feistiness is partly the product of temperament, but also of a painful childhood. Becoming aware of the trauma she experienced in her early years has given me compassion for her and the many women Eights I have had the privilege to know—each of them with a different version of the same struggle for survival.

My mother was still a little kid when she decided that people were not to be trusted. Sooner or later, they would hurt or betray her.

Sadly, she first learned that lesson at home.

My mom grew up in a well-to-do family on Long Island. Her home looked better from the outside than from the inside. Her father was a successful CEO of a large manufacturing company who was beloved in the community. He was also a violent rage-aholic who terrorized her and her four siblings.

"Every night at six, we would peek through the curtains to catch a glimpse of our father as he walked home from work," my mother once confided. "We could tell what kind of mood he was in from the look on his face and the way he walked. If he was smiling and walking easy, we knew we were safe. But if he was scowling and marching down the sidewalk, we would run and hide in the attic."

Her harrowing childhood left my mother feeling vulnerable, and vulnerable is not a feeling she enjoys. If she wanted to survive, she would have to become strong and powerful.

It saddens me to think that my mom internalized the message so early in life that she was the only person she could trust to watch out for her. It's a burden she has carried for ninety-three years.

See: The Eight's Origin Story

My mother didn't speak in full sentences until she was five years old.[1] Today, we know that a meaningful percentage of late-talker kids later prove to be incredibly bright and accomplished. If you don't believe me, ask Albert Einstein. Heck, he didn't speak in full sentences until he was five![2] But in 1933, late bloomers were considered "slow" and often got bullied. So in grade school, my mother learned that home wasn't the only unsafe place.

"One day in kindergarten another little girl and I were playing on the swings after school when her mother came over, took her daughter by the hand, and said 'I don't want you playing with retards.' I had never heard that word before but I could tell from the look on her face that it meant something was horribly wrong with me," she recalled. "That girl must have told the whole class what her mother said, because next day every kid in school was calling me that dreadful word. The taunting didn't let up until I finally started talking later that year. And once I started, I never stopped."

Knowing my mother and a little bit about psychology, I suspect that it was around this time that she internalized two messages. The first was, "Don't trust anyone. They will betray you and break your heart." The second was, "The world crushes the weak. If you don't want to end up at the mercy of the crowd, then you have to stand up and fight for yourself."

And that's what my mother did. She fought.

By the time she was in high school, she'd earned a reputation for being strongheaded and outspoken. The nuns at her Catholic high school told her she was too loud, too bossy, too opinionated, too sure of herself. *Too everything.*

"I always needed to take hold of the reins of my life," she told me over coffee one day, "but my friends loved my fearlessness and the way I took charge of things. So they were always pushing me toward leadership. In my junior year my parents sent me to a new school. Only one month in—before I even knew all my classmates' names—they made me president of the student body. Heck, I didn't even run for the dumb office—they *handed* me the job," she said laughing.

When I asked her what made people think she was a natural leader, my mother playfully poked her finger at me and said, "Because I get things *done.*" In many ways, my mother was a textbook example of the bold, fearless spirit that characterizes most Eights. Strong-willed, she channeled her anger into accomplishing things.

As with every type, the Eight's is a combination of nature and nurture—or, in some cases, a lack of nurture.[3] The danger in my mother's childhood home shaped her take-charge personality, her need to control others and the environment, her fierce self-determination, and her single-minded resolve to overcome any adversity. My mom rose to the challenge of taking care of herself. God bless her.

Not all Eights have difficult childhoods, but many do. Like most Eights, my mom came to craft her broken story around the fears she suffered as a child. Whether they are in real danger or simply perceive it that way, Eights learn very early that innocence is dangerous and they can't trust anyone without overwhelming evidence of loyalty.

Many Eights bury the painful feelings of their pasts and create a tough persona capable of withstanding anything life dishes out. Some overcome problems at home by being leaders at school, getting kudos for their grit and determination. Many Eight children are driven, but it's not quite the same way that other types are driven: it's not to be admired for their success (like Threes) or to satisfy an inner perfectionism (like Ones). Rather, Eights believe they need to be large and in charge. They tell themselves that they must conquer the world before it turns on them and disintegrates into the chaos they often experienced in their childhood.

Children who grow up in war zones or gang-ridden inner cities—where you can't afford to show weakness or cry—often become Eights. Some parents even reinforce this message, pushing vulnerable young Eights into situations where they have to prove themselves, tough it out, or fight back. Similarly, some Eights form because of the stories they tell themselves about how they think they must be in order to compete with siblings for mom and dad's attention. Unfortunately, some parents perpetuate this kind of unhealthy sibling rivalry by playing favorites or using their children to meet their own unmet emotional needs.

Tough and resilient, they develop a dauntlessness and confidence in their own abilities, certain that they need to be able to rely on themselves at all times. They gravitate toward (or are thrust into) leadership early on. Some have conflict with authority figures, especially if they perceive those authority figures as incompetent—like my mother's early observation that her father's capricious behavior made him not just unreliable, but dangerous. It's not necessarily that Eight kids want to control others, though some do; it's more that they don't want others to control *them*.

Own: The Strength and Shadow of the Eight

Real and perceived threats in childhood give birth to the oppositional energy that dominates the life of most Eights. Preemptive anger is an Eight's natural response to our imperfect, dangerous world. By the time Eights mature and reach young adulthood, they've become so entrenched in their approach to life that they begin to subconsciously use aggression—even combat—as a way to defend themselves against a hostile world. Ironically, they can become contentious as a way to stay connected to people they care about. Conflict can actually become their way of expressing intimacy.

Eights earn their anger honestly. After years of denying their own childhood weaknesses, not getting their needs met, and fending off the aggression of others, it's no wonder that some grow up to become aggressive themselves—combative, bull-headed, and intimidating.

On the other hand, Eights can be fiercely protective and coach others on how they should fight harder. They may question or criticize others for not handling situations the way they would: *You can't let him walk all over you like that! Get in his face!* Unskillful Eights who are stuck in their old story do not tend to apologize, or at least not easily. Even the occasional olive branch that's meant to say *I'm sorry* is often worded in the negative, blaming the other person for being too sensitive and getting offended.

Eights who lack self-awareness don't seek forgiveness—they won't own their offense, feel genuine remorse for how they've hurt another, or try to rebuild trust. Instead, they ask forgiveness for what others blame them for, not for what they see in themselves and are vulnerable enough to admit. It's almost as if they're saying *Too bad you can't handle someone as powerful as I am.* In other words, their own strength relies on another's weakness—much as the Eight likely experienced as a child.

No wonder many people find Eights so domineering and confrontational. They are Teflon at repelling anything that threatens to pierce their armor and force them to feel weak and vulnerable. While such exchanges may cause their family and friends to avoid bringing up potential land mine topics, Eights would rather walk right into them. Again, they love the direct, honest-'til-it-hurts approach. In fact, they're often baffled when others get offended and become excited when someone takes the bait to parry with them. They respect others who relate to people the same way they do. Any other response is considered weakness.

The weapon Eights created from their own weaknesses to fight their way forward when growing up quickly becomes a barrier in adulthood, an impenetrable defense system. Similar to underdeveloped Fives, these unhealthy Eights create a story requiring withdrawal from relationships because people can't be trusted. They become preoccupied with evidence that proves them right and reinforces their power over others. In short, they become scary loners.

Other ways of relating, requiring vulnerability and compromise, unconsciously frighten Eights with the possibility that they might fall victim to circumstances beyond their control again. Attempting to relate to others without control can cause great anxiety because it requires ongoing practice and conscious revision of the story they've been stuck in, the one that's become their armor as well as their security blanket.

Awaken: Counting the Cost

The take-no-prisoners story my mother concocted as a child worked well for her, until it didn't. Don't get me wrong—my mother never sat in a therapeutic drum circle and worked through her "childhood issues," nor did she know anything about the "any-a-gram." Consequences pushed her into discovering a new way of moving through the world. Replacing the old mantra "do others before they do you" came a new script: "Do for others and it will be done for you."

Here's what happened.

In the mid–1960s, my father's alcoholism and deteriorating mental health hit an all-time low. Unemployed, he was in and out of hospitals for alcohol-related health problems and suicidal depression. To put food on the table for her four children, my mother went to work as a secretary in a small publishing company. Little did the poor guy who hired her know that she would one day replace him. My gutsy mother quickly rose through the ranks in a male-dominated industry to become the vice president and publisher of her company.

She did this by learning from experience that fear of vulnerability and its "never let them see you cry" philosophy got in her way. So she changed her MO. Instead of fighting for herself, she began fighting for others—by caring for them.

In her new management role, my mother did something no other publisher in her industry had ever done. Rather than hiring salesmen, she hired and trained a team of ten women to make cold calls to prospective advertisers.

Not only did my mother create the first all-women's sales team in her industry's history, she staffed it with those who might otherwise have had trouble finding jobs in the early seventies. She employed weary single mothers struggling to hold their families together, women who were recovering from drinking or drug problems, caregivers of aging parents or grandchildren. They sat at rows of desks stretching down a long room, phones ringing off the hook. My mother would come out of her office to walk the line of desks, rallying the troops. When one of them generated a sale, she rang a call bell on her desk and the other women cheered and rang theirs as well.

But my mother's interest in these women extended well beyond what they produced for her. If they were in a custody battle, she showed up in court as their character witness. If they fell off the wagon, she helped them get back on their feet. When they needed a loan to pay for a child's schooling, she fronted them money. When they laughed, she laughed. When they cried, she cried.

Those women loved my mother, affectionately calling her "Fast Annie" and referring to themselves as "Fast Annie's Girls." Year after year they shattered sales records, and her division became the most profitable in her company.

My mother retired over three decades ago. To this day, my mom's "girls" still ring up "Fast Annie" to ask how she's doing or seek her advice. The spreading influence of my mother's awakening—from a hardened aggression to return of a childlike innocence through an earned intimacy—illuminates the Eight's transformation from passion to virtue, shadow to strength.

Rewrite: Craft Your New Story

My mother's story is unique, but it's also one that will sound pretty familiar to Challengers and those who love them. On the path from the Passion of the Eight (lust) to its Virtue (innocence), you have to practice the steps of SOAR: first, seeing your "origin story" and how past experiences of weakness may have contributed to your default need to appear strong at all times; second, owning the Eight's shadow side of controlling others through aggression; and, third, awakening to what the cost will be if you continue your current patterns of behavior. You learn to see the causes (what you're thinking and feeling) and effects (how you behave and relate) objectively enough to identify what's going on.

This is where the Enneagram helps. On a large scale, it identifies these patterns and helps you step back and look at what's been going on. Knowing your type provides a way of knowing your story, and knowing your story means you can learn to change it. So often, though, we tend to be so unconsciously entangled in our stories that it's hard to see the forest for the trees. We're used to seeing the world and other people, and our responses to them, as normal and familiar. And, as I mentioned in an earlier chapter, some people even use the Enneagram as a tool to reinforce their old story. They may go through the first two steps—they know their type and recognize its typical patterns of behavior—but they stop there. They stay asleep to the way that old story is driving their lives, and by closing their eyes they deprive themselves of any possibility of a rewrite. Creating a new and better narrative, however, requires us to see what we've been willing to overlook.

So, the first order of business when changing your story is simple: Don't do what you usually do. Remember the Ignatian idea of *agere contra,* or acting against. It's the spiritual discipline of not doing what you would usually do. *Agere contra* means not going through the motions of your usual default behaviors.

You do this by cultivating awareness of what you usually do that you haven't realized you're doing. You have to develop skills of self-observation. You know how you tend to go on mental autopilot when you're driving to work or school or somewhere you regularly visit? Then one day your usual route gets blocked, and you're suddenly forced to pay attention and take an entirely unfamiliar detour to get to your destination. You notice the trees along the highway, the shops just past the traffic light, the sound of a siren.

No longer on default, you're forced into the present moment.

That's what being self-aware and hitting pause is all about.

Once you've taken a time-out from the way you usually live your old story, you make a different choice. I like to think of this as the difference between reacting and responding. Reactions make me think of Newton's third law from science class: *For every action, there is an equal and opposite reaction.* If you pick an apple from a tree, then the branch will recoil when the stem breaks. If you punch someone, then your fist will bounce away from the point of contact. (Please don't try this as an experiment.)

In childhood, all of us pick up faulty beliefs that support and perpetuate the old story we drag into adulthood. To realize deep inner transformation, every type needs to see, challenge, and rid themselves of these taken-for-granted beliefs that sustain their archaic story. A few of the Eight's self-limiting beliefs might include:

- Being vulnerable is far too dangerous.
- I am invincible.
- I can do what I want.
- When the going gets tough, the tough take charge.
- Weakness will not be tolerated.
- No one can tell me what to do.

Notice: the story Eights tell themselves about who they are and how the world works is in direct opposition to the story of a loving, gracious God. Do people need to adopt a defended, aggressive posture to defend themselves against the possibility of betrayal and pain? Does God equate vulnerability with weakness and expect us to do the same? Nope.

In my novel *Chasing Francis* I discuss Thomas Aquinas's description of two kinds of souls.[4] The *magna animi* is the large soul that bravely opens itself to the world. It's where we get the word "magnanimous." The *pusilla animi* is the small soul that guards itself against the world. It sees others as potential threats, enemies waiting to pounce. It's where we get the word "pusillanimous." Eights need to see that adopting a pusillanimous posture isn't strength— it's faintheartedness masquerading as toughness.

Dominican priest Simon Tugwell described Christians as those who ideally live a "radically unprotected life" in cruciform shape. They dare to outstretch their arms and bravely expose their hearts to the world the way Jesus did on the cross.[5] They open themselves to the pain and sorrow of the world. This is the life we're called to live.

If you're an Eight, you will take particular joy in what I'm about to tell you: You have control over the choices you make every single day. You are the narrator of your own story. No matter how confining your circumstances, there are always options. When you feel anger, you don't have to power up and lash out. When you're stressed, you don't have to withdraw, accuse, blame, or deflect. When you're hurt, you don't have to bury your pain behind a stoic façade of emotional control or go on the offensive. Assume control of your new story; don't let your old story control you.

That was appealing to my friend Dr. Sasha Shillcutt, an Eight who first learned about the Enneagram when she was taking an executive leadership course in health care at Harvard.[6] "Oh, here we go," she groaned when she was given the Enneagram test. "Every time I take a personality test or assessment, it's going to tell me all of the things I don't like about myself." Instruments like the Myers-Briggs seemed static; that test could tell her which of the sixteen types she was but didn't allow for movement or growth. What intrigued her about the Enneagram was that it had a built-in path for growth and change. It didn't just label her behavior or predict how she might behave in a stressful environment like an operating room; it taught her that she had choices.

"It was the first time I took an internal assessment of myself and didn't feel bad, didn't feel like I was too much of something," Sasha explained. "Because as an Eight, I'm a lot. I don't have a dimmer switch. And instead of feeling bad and toning down who I am, I get to choose. I get to choose whether I choose the stress path or the growth path. Or I get to choose whether I will lean this way or that way."

What got Sasha excited about the Enneagram, as an Eight, was that it could give her options and release her grip on her old defense mechanisms. She saw it as a tool of empowerment, one that enabled her to no longer be controlled by her own personality. She didn't have to react to situations in one stereotyped way but could use the Enneagram as a tool for learning other approaches.

That's key. Instead of reacting, you can *respond*.

When I consider the difference between reacting and responding, I think about the Holocaust and Viktor Frankl. I first read his classic *Man's Search for Meaning* as a freshman in college. It blew my mind that not only did he survive a Nazi concentration camp during World War II, a place of horrors that claimed the lives of most of his other family members, but that he somehow found meaning, hope, and strength amidst such trauma. That's a remarkable story revision. Afterward, he spent the rest of his life as a psychiatrist, author, speaker, and humanitarian, best known for his method of psychotherapy known as logotherapy.

Frankl believed that our ability to recognize and exercise choices about how to respond to what happens to us is the foundation of human freedom. This inner freedom allowed him to endure the seemingly hopeless circumstances of his torturous captivity. Even as a prisoner in a concentration camp, where he seemingly had no freedom, "there were always choices to make," he wrote. He knew prisoners who walked through the huts to comfort other men, even though they were themselves suffering, and gave them their last piece of bread. "They may have been few in number, but they offer sufficient proof that everything can be taken from a man but one thing: the last of the human freedoms—to choose one's attitude in any given set of circumstances, to choose one's own way."[7] Frankl realized he could merely react and give up hope or he could look at the situation differently and find room to respond.

Regardless of type, we can create space to respond to anything and everything that happens to us as well. While we can't control certain circumstances, especially those involving the decisions of others, we can control how we regard those events and any actions we take or don't take. Once we realize there's this space available for us to stand in, then we can own our freedom to choose between responding to life and reacting to it.

Changing our story is tied to the process of realizing that there *is* a space—and then taking steps to widen that gap between action and reaction so we can live mind*fully* instead of mind*lessly*. Waking up from our scripted trance, we realize we no longer have to sleep-walk as a character trapped in a destructive story. We wake up and consider new and different possibilities. We create a crossroads and turn in a new direction. We claim authorship of our story rather than mere participation.

Once we realize we have choices, then we can reframe our perspective. If you're growing in awareness of how you usually behave and want a new story, then you can choose to replace what you subconsciously have accepted with an update on what's true now as opposed to what was true in your formative experiences. For evolved Eights, the world may still be a hostile place, but they learn to recognize that it's also a place of beauty, joy, and love. They realize they can risk going off-duty sometimes to trust others, to experience rest, to acknowledge their vulnerability. Evolved Eights understand that vulnerability is not weakness.

When we cultivate awareness of our type tendencies, we learn to refrain from playing the same role in our old story, to create space so we can respond instead of react, and to reframe our perspective into a better story.

Ideas for the Eight's New Story

No type has it any easier than another when it comes to revising old stories into new ones. Every human being has to befriend themselves in the process of maturing and transforming into who they were made to be. This isn't merely telling yourself self-help slogans and can-do maxims during times of pain, hardship, and struggle. Befriending yourself requires the kind of acceptance and patience we would share with anyone we love who was hurting. Remember: Eights are moving toward a Virtue of innocence, of childlike trust in goodness. Let innocence be a North Star of sorts as you consider how to rewrite your story.

For Eights like my mother and Sasha, this often resembles a well-developed, healthy Two. If you're familiar with the Enneagram's arrows—the direction markers leading toward and away from your own number on the system's diagram—you'll see that Eights embody the best characteristics of the Two when they are feeling secure. They grow comfortable with acknowledging their own emotions and needs even as they offer transparency and reciprocity to others. Such emotional healing may require grief work to address the losses of childhood and the lingering wounds of traumatic violations. As Eights begin writing their new story, they reconnect to their hearts and realize what it means to be awake in the present instead of always on guard because of the past.

Twos are very aware of how they come across to others and strive to honor other people's feelings. Think about what it would look like for a powerful Eight to put that sensitivity into practice. Aware of their tendencies to default into anger, Eights in new stories learn to check themselves before communicating in moments of tension, stress, and conflict. Like healthy Twos, they become better attuned to the feelings of others. They no longer fly off the handle and they find ways to build bridges instead of burning them. They build intimacy through tenderness rather than animosity. They accept that new challenges will come and go without triggering old defense systems. If you're an Eight who wants to rewrite your story, practice showing respect, kindness, and patience when talking to others as opposed to being confrontational by default. Come up with gentler strategies *before* you go into situations where you tend to dominate.

Agere contra is a useful tool for Eights. As you communicate, show your appreciation and gratitude to others on a regular basis, especially those people who support, encourage, and believe in you. Learn to appreciate that they do things differently than you and that this does not make them weak. In fact, they might teach you something—and in your Virtue state of innocence, you are more open to learning from others.

Eights who are rewriting their stories should realize that most people just don't enjoy bantering, sparring, and fighting as much as you do—especially those related to you. You may find battle therapeutic, a ritual clearing of the air. Others find it stressful and overpowering. So, as you seek to rewrite your story, don't lean into conflict generation as your default mode of being in the world. Take your emotional cues from the people around you.

Along those same lines, don't attack others who criticize you, even if their expressions are inappropriate or hurtful. Consider the basis for what they're saying and whether it contains any truth. Own your responsibility for insisting on doing things your way, and admit your mistakes. Healthy Eights not only offer criticism but take it well themselves. To help you do this, create an inner circle of people with whom you can be direct and honest who reciprocate these qualities with you. Solicit regular feedback from them, perhaps weekly, about how you're coming across, and *trust their input*. That's key. Listen to those trusted advisors and respond accordingly.

Remember that the most powerful leaders are actually the ones who choose to empower others, not to hoard all of the authority and decision-making for themselves. So, make an experiment of regularly deferring to others instead of automatically taking the lead. Try to say "Great, let's do it your way!" at least once a day and mean it. Doubt your own certainty that you are always right, and take seriously the idea that someone else might be right. Let go of being the one who makes most of the decisions. It's going to seem scary to surrender control like this, so begin by supporting the leadership of someone you particularly trust and respect. Look for ways to mentor and encourage those who look to you as an example. Gradually, as you see that some of those experiments are successful, you'll feel the freedom that comes from *not* having to run the show.

Finally, regularly check in with yourself. Recognize when you're acting tough to compensate for feeling weak or vulnerable. Tell yourself in a compassionate voice, "I have fallen back into the old story. Do I want to stay there? Will this end well?" Remind yourself that it's okay not to feel strong all the time. When you get angry, acknowledge your anger in the moment, preferably in a way that's appropriate, constructive, and reasonable instead of holding it in and harboring grudges that grow over time. Don't concoct elaborate revenge scenarios to get back at the people who've hurt you, which is a hallmark of an unhealthy Eight.[8] A major part of rewriting your story is the ability to move on.

Eights in their new stories make brilliant leaders because they care more about serving those following them than exercising power over them. Think Harriet Tubman leading the Underground Railroad. Winston Churchill during the Blitz. Or Martin Luther King Jr. galvanizing America behind the civil rights movement.

Eights want to be in charge. But if they're willing to leave their old story, they can expect a smoother ride. They can enjoy living in a new story that draws on the full range of human emotions and strengths of their true self.

4

The Nine's Story

An Awakening for the Peacemaker

"You find peace not by rearranging the circumstances of your life, but by realizing who you are at the deepest level."
—Eckhart Tolle

I first met Mike McHargue a few years ago at the Wild Goose Festival, where I heard him give an amazing talk on the intersection of science and faith. Little did I know we would become friends and that he would one day open my eyes to the fascinating inner terrain of Enneagram Nines.

Mike developed his Nine story early. There was an authority figure in his family who terrified him, and that experience taught Mike the lesson that most Nines internalize from childhood: conflict is scary, anger must be avoided, and to stay connected to other people it's vital to stay attuned to their moods and go with the flow.[1]

He developed a sensitive antenna "to forecast emotional storms on the horizon and prevent them," as he puts it. His own anger frightened him, which is a common issue for Nines. What if he erupted and became like this authority figure? So, he stuffed it down into what he calls his "Nine basement," where it could never explode. His job was to keep the peace.

Mike is a.k.a. "Science Mike" of *The Liturgists* podcast. He's a bestselling author, a consultant about science for film and television, and a sought-after speaker. But, when he was a kid, fading into the shadows was a successful defense strategy. Invisibility helped him manage his world.

Mike was sometimes bullied by other kids, which he handled by pointing that finely tuned antenna on the bullies to learn what made them tick. He figured out which of his behaviors might set them off and what might make him less of a target so he could disappear from their radar. What worked best for him was blending in with the wallpaper. Socially, he wasn't aiming for acceptance—that was too high a bar. For him, a great success was "just to be ignored."

Mike's belief that it was up to him to maintain harmony is a common element in the story many Nines create about what they must do to survive. They learn quickly that the world is an unsettling, conflict-filled place. Consequently, Nines tell themselves they need to do and say whatever they can to *escape* such drama and to *conform* to whatever behavior seems to prevent blowups from happening. Most Nines get along fine with others until their siblings, friends, or family members cause conflict. Then Nines fall asleep to their anger and lose touch with it in order to maintain the peace.

For many Nines, this pattern of avoiding conflict and slumbering through their own emotional life continues well into adulthood. For Mike, a wake-up moment came when he was in his thirties and going to therapy after a faith transition. "I didn't believe what I used to and I found myself kind of ejected from my faith community, which was incredibly traumatic," he says. The therapist asked him to describe another time when he had been rejected, so he found himself rehashing "in clinical terms and excruciating detail" the various acts of bullying that he'd experienced in childhood.

As he recounted the story, he felt no emotional investment in what had happened, which made him feel good about himself, imagining that he had processed that old pain completely.

But then she asked, "Well, how did that make you feel?"

It was a simple enough question, but it hit Mike in an unexpected way. "I felt like I'd passed by a hallway in my house with a door that I'd never seen. And I put my hand up to the door, and it was just . . . It felt as hot as the sun behind that door, like the house was on fire behind the door."

He told the therapist that the question made him uncomfortable. "If I talk to you about how I feel, I'm either going to yell or sob," he cautioned.

"Why would that be a bad thing?"

"Well, those are really wasteful emotions. They're very unpleasant to experience, and they don't accomplish anything."

"Do you think it's healthy just to bottle those feelings down?" she persisted. "What if you just told me how you felt? And if you cry, that's okay."

So, Mike started to describe his feelings but couldn't get a word out before he sobbed for a brief moment and then immediately stopped. His eyes dried up.

"What just happened?" the therapist wanted to know.

Mike realized his body was doing exactly what he had taught it to do when he'd been bullied so many years before: *don't cry, because that will only encourage the bullies to keep beating you.*

The problem was that the old story that had worked for him in childhood in protecting him from the bullies was holding him back in adulthood from experiencing his anger and sadness. He had reached his thirties and was unable to cry, even at the death of a family member, so there were decades of numbness to undo.

"I spent several months in the therapist's office letting go of thirty-plus years of grief," he told me. "Once I was able to do that, it was this briny river coming out of my soul that made me feel clean."

Mike was waking up to his grief and anger.

See: The Nine's Origin Story

Mike's emotional situation is typical of Nines. On the one hand, they are like a Kansas resident sheltering in the storm cellar during a tornado. They learn to read the emotional weather patterns of others and then hunker down when a crisis cannot be averted. On the other hand, they're numb to their own weather patterns. They've often stuffed their own feelings and desires for so long that they don't even know what those feelings and desires are.

Growing up, Nines formulate a story that goes like this: *The world threatens my inner harmony. The important people in my life react to circumstances and to each other in ways that frighten and unsettle me. In order to survive, I'd better not rock the boat. I have to avoid conflicts and keep the peace. Better to become invisible than to voice my needs, feelings, and preferences.*

Their narrative is fueled by accommodation and inner peace: I'm okay as long as everyone else is okay.

What keeps the Nine's broken story alive is their unconscious, mistaken beliefs. If Nines want to undo their old story and make space for a new one, they have to bring these faulty beliefs into conscious awareness and interrogate them. A few of the unconscious, taken-for-granted beliefs that keep Nines trapped in their old story include:

- What I want doesn't really matter.
- Attention from others is okay as long as it's not focused on me for too long.
- Everything is okay if there is no conflict.
- I can get my needs met by others through forgetting myself, my ideas, and my agenda.
- It's best not to be too affected by life.
- I'm a *nice* person who doesn't get angry.
- I'm okay as long as everyone else is okay.
- I need to make people happy, even if it means sacrificing my own priorities.

Nines are usually the low-maintenance kids every parent wants. They've been called the "sweethearts of the Enneagram" and can often showcase the best qualities of the other eight types, merging with the priorities and opinions of other people in order to avoid conflict. Nines intuitively seem to know how to read other people and adapt accordingly.

These kids don't make waves. But they often feel like others don't pay attention to them or acknowledge their perspectives, opinions, or desires. Other people seem to them to have more passionate opinions about what they want, so Nines decide not to upset the applecart by asserting themselves.

Family therapist Chris Gonzalez started down his Nine path quite consciously as a kid, even though he didn't know anything about the Enneagram at that time or have a name for what he was doing.[2] "I have an older brother who is attracted to conflict, and I watched how that went for him and decided that wasn't the way I wanted to go," he says. His brother was a good person, but he left behind a "wake of destruction," which left a deep impression. "I decided, 'I'm going to do the opposite of that. I'm going to get as quiet as I can be. I'm going to pass for invisible. I see where conflict can get somebody, and I don't want that.'"

In fact, Chris has started writing a memoir called, appropriately enough, *Invisibility Lessons*. He hasn't finished it, though—it's "in a file somewhere with a hundred other stories that I'm going to get to someday, obviously someday."

What Chris is half-jokingly acknowledging here is that Nines often have a hard time finishing things. They don't have the Eight's drive for control, the One's fear of doing things imperfectly, or the Three's need to succeed. The Passion for Nines is sloth, which we tend to associate with physical laziness, but that's only one small part of it. It's true that some Nines seem to have less stamina than other people and can even check out in certain situations.

When Mike McHargue was on an overseas trip with some friends, for example, it became the joke of the group that he could fall asleep absolutely anywhere. In a noisy café, they had only been sitting down for maybe five minutes before he leaned his head back against the wall and nodded off. He made himself so invisible that the group left without him, not realizing until later that he was still fast asleep in his chair in the restaurant.

In Mike's case, that's a funny story. But, for many Nines, the need to numb or zone out periodically, and the tendency to procrastinate, is related to their inability to figure out what they want. Their learned pattern of tamping down their own desires as children often means that, when they are adults, it's hard for them to seal the deal, develop their own gifts in a meaningful way, or follow each step toward a goal. Chris and Mike are exceptions in that they've overcome this pattern and gone after their dreams, becoming highly successful in their chosen arenas. For every Chris and Mike, though, there are plenty of dozing Nines who don't quite know what their dreams are or have the first idea about how to pursue them.

It can take Nines forever to make a decision, and they sometimes miss deadlines, procrastinate, or "narcotize" when faced with stress. That doesn't necessarily mean they're doing drugs but rather that they have lots of strategies to tune out the world. They might binge on ice cream, play video games, or spend an entire weekend on the couch watching reruns of *Seinfeld*.

Both my wife, Anne, and daughter, Maddie, are healthy Nines, and yet I can always tell when they're having a tough time. We'll be doing something together that they enjoy, like cooking or listening to a podcast, or playing cornhole (yup, we do that a lot), and yet they're mentally and emotionally checked out. When they push in the clutch and disengage their mental transmission, I know this sometimes means they're angry, frustrated, or ramping up to face a hard decision. When this happens, I gently ask them if there's something going on beneath the surface (sometimes that question goes over well, sometimes not so much).

Some Nines' numbing behaviors can even involve otherwise healthy activities, like disappearing for hours to hike in the woods (many Nines love nature), reading novels, or exercising. Whatever the activity, if the point of it is to tamp down unacknowledged desire or anger or run away from conflict, it can become part of the Nine's defense mechanism—narcotizing.

At bottom, Nines are afraid that if they assert their own agenda, it will compete with the desires, ambitions, or dreams of another person with whom they don't want to lose a connection. Sticking to the script they've memorized, these Nines lack initiative because change—even positive change—is scary and requires that they burn calories. They prefer the devils they know.

If they don't wake up and make the choice to inhabit a new story, Nines can end up with a life that's unworthy of their gifts and spirit.

Own: The Strength and Shadow of the Nine

I've noticed that Nines often have a very hard time settling on their Enneagram type. "Well, I can kind of see myself in that," they'll say when presented with the creativity of a Four, the helpfulness of a Two, or the loyalty of a Six. In an unevolved Nine, this happens because of their ability to identify with every type's point of view. They haven't done the work of individuating, preferring to draft behind stronger personalities or the more passionate opinions of the group. It's just easier that way.

Audrey Assad, a fantastic singer I admire, says that when she was younger, she used to fuse with other people and that it was not a healthy dynamic.[3] "We mistake enmeshment for empathy," she says. If she wasn't fully anchored in herself, she became "a barnacle going down with the submarine," overly involved in other people's lives and dramas. Her emotional sensitivity to other people's pain can be a strength, but her Nine tendency toward merging with others was also a problem—as she puts it, it could even become "vampiric."

But healthy Nines, those who have shed the old story that their desires and preferences don't matter, manifest beautiful strengths as they begin to flourish. Nines who are in a new story are amazing. They let life unfold naturally, offering others the freedom and space to grow in their own time and at their own pace. They're quick to love, slow to judge, and they rarely ask to be recognized for the effort they put in to caring for other people—which I can tell you is considerable.

One of those evolved Nines is my friend William Paul Young, author of the bestselling novel *The Shack*, who says he didn't feel angry until he was thirty-eight and his life fell apart.[4] That implosion was actually a good thing because there was a lot he should have been angry about all along, such as serious childhood trauma that he had never allowed himself to grieve.

Now that he is in a healthy space, Paul has an almost mystical quality that I love, his Nine tolerance extending to everyone around him. Just as I said that unhealthy Nines can be hard to type because they merge in self-abnegating ways with other people, *healthy* Nines can actually be difficult to type as well, but for a different reason: they have beautifully integrated the strengths of the other numbers. Paul is like that. Today, he feels anger sometimes—fury, even—and allows it to fuel his creativity. "I don't want that fury to be damaging to the truth of human beings," he says now. "I want it to be exposing the corruption and the perpetration of the injustice that we do one to another, and to ourselves. I feel more fury in my life now than I've ever felt, but I'm not burdened by it. It is to me evidence of the health that has happened in my own heart." He can cry and he can feel and he can even decide where to go for dinner, which is something that as an unevolved Nine he had a difficult time doing. Paul is owning the strength of the Nine.

Awaken: Counting the Cost

Paul was fortunate: in his late thirties he woke up, even though it was deeply painful at the time. Other Nines continue slumbering, staggering through each day as if through a minefield, committed to avoiding any explosive steps that might shatter their inner sense of peace. Worst case, they continue acquiescing to the decisions of others at the expense of their own sense of identity. Trapped in their old story, they say, "It doesn't matter to me as much as it does to you—whatever you want is fine," while inside, perhaps subconsciously, their true self becomes angrier and more stubborn. Left unchecked, undeveloped Nines may seem like pleasant, easygoing people at first but then quickly become passive-aggressive as their resentment grows over the way they accommodate others to keep the peace.

Sometimes it takes something dramatic to get Nines to wake up to their anger. My friend Seth Abram, an Enneagram podcaster who is a Nine, once flew into an uncharacteristic rage when he witnessed a family member being horribly mistreated.[5] The emotion was so strong that he had to get out of the house, so he drove to a nearby parking lot where he could yell and pound on the steering wheel.

"I haven't had many moments like this," he says. "What anger feels like in my body is that I could pick up a car and throw it across the room, like it weighs nothing. That is exactly what I felt like in that moment, like I had the potential of ten men. It's just such an opposite of what the Nine personality usually looks like."

Seth called his best friend to help him process the intensity. He knew based on ten years of close friendship that this guy was a safe person who could handle seeing this side of Seth, but it was a risk. "This was a version of me that he'd never seen at all. There'd never been any sign of it. But here I was, yelling and screaming for fifteen minutes straight at the top of my lungs."

Later, after he calmed down, Seth called his friend back, wondering whether he might have crossed a line.

"What was that like for you?" Seth asked, apologetically. "I hope that wasn't offensive, but I needed to get it out."

"You don't have to apologize, man," his friend responded. "I have never seen you more alive."

What an affirmation for a Nine. Seth had two incredible gifts from this experience. First, he learned that, although his anger was frightening, it was also empowering. "It's the true meaning of embodiment: I'm experiencing every cell, every ounce, every aspect of my physicality all at once. I feel way bigger than I actually am." And, second, his anger was actually beautiful to someone he loved. This friend could not only absorb the waves of Seth's emotions but could see them as holy.

Rewrite: Craft Your New Story

As we've seen, the Passion for Nines is sloth. If you're familiar at all with the behavior of sloths in the wild, you'll know that they are slow movers and heavy sleepers. In fact, one sloth variety is so slow and moves so seldom that algae can grow on its coat. That's actually an advantage, since sloths are conflict-avoidant and hide best from predators when they blend in with the green leaves of the trees where they make their homes. Sloths mostly eat leaves and plants within their reach, but if an obliging insect happens along, why, they'll eat that too, as long as catching it doesn't require a lot of effort. They're not picky about their food or their companions or their environment. They're not picky about much of anything, really. Some spend their entire lives chilling out in the exact same tree they were born in.[6]

You can see why the sloth is the perfect mascot for the sleep-walking Nine, whose old story involves hiding from conflict, staying in one place to avoid change, and acting like they're fine with whatever's going on around them. An unskillful Nine's inertia is a wonder to behold. They're like the human embodiment of Newton's first law, which states that an object at rest wants to stay at rest "unless compelled to change its state by the action of an external force."[7]

The challenge for the Nine is to move from the Passion of sloth to the Virtue of right action. Therein lies the hope of a real awakening, a chance to rewrite their story. The problem, as Newton's law of inertia makes clear, is that Nines aren't inclined to get moving on their own unless some external force acts upon them.

I want to point out that all nine Enneagram types are going against the grain as they implement *agere contra* and move from their Passion to their Virtue, but starting this process may be even harder for Nines because the act of moving itself runs against their natural tendencies. Rewriting their story is not merely acting differently than they normally would, as we saw with the Eight; rather, it's the choice of acting at all. For Nines, *agere contra* starts with the mere decision to do something.

But the results are so worth the effort. When Nines begin waking up, they're individuating and coming into focus. When they do, they're often amazed at how much other people enjoy discovering who they really are when they're not automatically agreeing with them or checked out—like Seth experienced when he completely lost his temper. These Nines realize the old story doesn't hold true because their opinions and preferences *do* matter to those around them. Their friends, family, and co-workers will not reject them or shift into combat when they voice their decisions or express anger. And, even when others disagree or a conflict develops, awakened Nines realize that it's okay. They see how much they've mentally exaggerated the potential fallout from facing a problem with someone head-on. While it may never feel entirely comfortable for them, they accept conflict as an unavoidable part of life for everyone.

A man I know told me two ways he's learned to change his old Nine story. The first is simply cultivating a stronger sense of his true self by doing things that require him to invest in himself. Nines can be lazy about self-development. For him, investing in himself includes taking guitar lessons, hiking at least once a month with a couple of friends from work, and leading the discussion on the next book at his twelve-step recovery group. Pursuing these activities means less time for watching TV, getting lost in meaningless tasks, and vegging out at home.

He also spends five to ten minutes each morning praying, meditating, or just being mindful of waking up, both literally and figuratively. This second practice helps him recognize the powerful difference his presence makes in the lives of others. "My wife gave me this coffee mug that says I'M SHOWING UP. It reminds me to pay attention. It's a literal wake-up call to think about how

I can avoid autopilot and contribute to a better world for the people around me." When I pressed him on what this looks like, he said that it's often forcing himself to notice when his mind begins to wander, retraining himself to stay in the moment rather than drift away.

Other Nines have told me that they, too, benefit from having a "totem," a reminder that refocuses their attention on the present moment. For some, it's as simple as a Post-it note on their bathroom mirror. Others wear a bracelet or necklace, carry a stone from a sacred place in their pocket, or hang a special photo or piece of art where they can see it throughout their day. There's nothing magical about any of these items—they're simply reminders to cut through the inertia and the clutter that Nines once allowed to pile up. These Nines use the objects to break through old default patterns throughout the day. When they feel themselves slipping away from the present moment, they let the totem break the spell and restore mindfulness to what and who is right in front of them.

Ideas for the Nine's New Story

New-story Nines are amazing people with so much to give. Their ability to see others' perspectives, to broker peace amidst opposing factions, and to extend kindness and compassion affords them unique status. They can identify with each of the other types even as they struggle to unleash the beauty of their true self. Like all the types, changing their story requires self-observation, intentionality, and action.

Here's an idea from Audrey Assad, to counteract her tendency to merge in an unhealthy way with others. When she feels herself doing this, she takes a breath and assesses the situation. "Where are my boundaries dissolving?" she asks. She then envisions a physical border around herself, a boundary that helps to preserve her individual identity. She can still help people, reaching across the border to empathize with a friend, but she retains her sense of self.

As Nines engage in the early steps of SOAR, one important activity for them is to make a list of all their default numbing strategies: surfing online, gaming (yes, crossword puzzles and Sudoku count), listening to podcasts, eating donuts, binge-watching HBO, or whatever. If you're a Nine, pay attention to when you slip away from being present and slide into these escapes. Choose one to work on eliminating. You're not going to conquer it all at once, but you will feel more powerful just by getting started.

Another strategy is to review your regular habits and routines and make at least one change that will remind you to change the story you've been telling yourself. Instead of, "I'm so lazy—I try to do laundry every week, but I'm never caught up," you might try, "Wednesdays are laundry days, and then I don't have to think about it the rest of the week." It may be helpful to involve a loved one in this process, particularly someone who depends on you to follow through with things. Then take right action.

Show up for others each day by doing what you've committed to do for them as efficiently as possible: arriving for work on time, enrolling your kids in the soccer camp they requested before the deadline, making the doctor's appointment, sending the email, attending the committee meeting *and* actively participating. Surprise them, and yourself, by doing what needs doing before someone nags you to. It will get easier over time. Remember Newton's law about inertia and how an object at rest wants to stay at rest? Well, that law also has a second part: an object in motion wants to stay in motion. Once you start taking regular steps to rewrite your old story, you'll be in motion, and *motion* will become the default mode that it takes precious energy to change.

Don't self-forget in this process as you learn to show up for others and interrupt the circuit on your default habit of checking out of life. You're not doing this just to keep other people happy or keep them from nagging you about doing the minimum to get by. You're doing this for you. One thing I've noticed about Nines who are spiritually asleep is that they routinely discount their own desires and anticipate that others will discount them too. Don't do that. Try practicing unconditional empathy for yourself. This is, in fact, how all types experience change, which we will continue to explore, but for Nines it's especially important. I'll never forget how Anne Bogel described her first dose of self-empathy.[8] Anne is a blogger, podcaster, author, and influencer for readers, authors, and book lovers. A classic Nine, she shared how her therapist once challenged her to respond to herself just as she would treat a teenager emerging from similar life events as those that shaped Anne's story.

"Do you know any sixteen-year-old girls?" the therapist asked. "Imagine this happening to them."

"Oh, those poor babies," Anne said, suddenly shocked by the possibility of accepting and comforting herself the same as she would for a daughter, a niece, or a friend. "It just totally changed the way that I understood the situation." Anne described how she wouldn't hesitate to counsel, mentor, and embrace others in need but always struggled to show similar kindness to herself. Some Nines find it helpful to imagine doing just that before acknowledging that they deserve the same compassion.

When they toss out their old stories, Nines often become in-credibly self-aware leaders. They embody a kind of wholeness and grounded soulfulness that combines the superpowers of the other eight types. They become prisms, not collectors, of others' stories, able to listen, accept, and offer insight in transcendent ways.

These Nines no longer overthink every decision or get lost in tangential distractions. They can use their incredible ability to see all sides of any given circumstance and let go of their old-story commitment to find the *best option*, which consumes an enormous amount of mental energy and can leave them exhausted and stuck. When Nines learn to stop ruminating, they can start spending time on things that bring more peace, love, and joy into their lives—and sharing these gifts with those around them.

5

The One's Story

*Radical Acceptance
for the Improver*

"Have no fear of perfection—you'll never reach it."
—Salvador Dali

I think Amy Julia Becker was probably born responsible. The oldest of four children, she would help her parents around the house, unloading the dishwasher without being asked. She took phone messages for her parents, got excellent grades in school, and never got in trouble. (It's hard for me to wrap my head around this kind of compliant behavior in a child. At school age I displayed symptoms of early onset oppositional behavior disorder.)

"A.J." (as she's known to her friends) also wanted to make the world a better place. In the fifth grade, she attended a school where the merry-go-round was deemed to be dangerous. Already responsible and proactive, she wasn't about to let that stand. "Well, we can fix that," A.J. told herself. She started a fund-raising campaign to fix the broken merry-go-round and bring it up to code so she and her classmates would have a safer playground.

She saw a problem, and she came up with a good solution. In the fifth grade.

A.J. is a One on the Enneagram, and like a lot of young Ones, she was remarkably mature as a child. These are often kids who inherently want to do the right thing, not simply in order to get along with others as a Nine might or to earn appreciation like a Two but *because* it's the right thing. Even if no one is watching, One kids tend to follow the rules and set a good example. They have high standards for the world and, most of all, for themselves.

But, for a fair number of Ones, those standards can become a painful burden. In A.J.'s case, her perfectionism contributed to an eating disorder in high school and college. Although she didn't pay much attention to makeup or hair, she was obsessive about not gaining a single pound. She recorded her food intake in a journal ("Apple. Salad. Frozen yogurt. Apple. Diet Coke.") and signed and dated a promise to herself that she would never eat more than 1,000 calories a day. "A covenant with the gods of thinness, the currency of beauty," as she put it in her beautiful memoir, *A Good and Perfect Gift.*[1]

It caught up with her. When she tried eating normally again, her body rejected the food, and she would throw up. She couldn't quite admit that she had an eating disorder. It wasn't bulimia because she wasn't actively doing anything to initiate the purging. "It was like, 'It's not my fault. I eat whatever,'" she described her attitude at the time.[2] She was diagnosed with *gastroparesis*, which is a paralyzed stomach that does not move food as quickly as it should, in her case, probably a result of the severely restricted diet she had previously undertaken.

"There was a sense of there being a lot of secrecy and shame," she said. She told others that the doctors had said she was sick and there was no cure. That was true, but the underlying eating disorder, which was "not about appearance so much as it was about control," was difficult to talk about. She had spent her life to that point tamping down anxiety and anger in an effort to stay in control.

"I remember telling a therapist, 'Oh no, I've never been angry.' Now, in retrospect, I'm like, Ding! Ding! Ding! There's a problem here."

Growth for A.J. has come by acknowledging when she experiences negative emotions and honoring the connection between her body, her emotions, and her mind. It has also happened through parenting, especially with her first child, Penny, who was born with a disability.

"We found out that she had Down syndrome two hours after she was born," A.J. said. "The word, the language, used around Down syndrome is imperfection, defect, and abnormality. I mean, the language itself speaks to that. I was really wrestling with my own perfectionism and my own set of expectations around her."

She hadn't realized it when she was pregnant with Penny, but she had come to motherhood with certain expectations, unvoiced but present. She wrote later:

It was as if having kids had become an equation: youth plus devotion to God plus education equaled a healthy and normal baby. As if taking a birthing class and reading baby books and

abstaining from alcohol and praying all guaranteed certain
things about our family. As if I were entitled to exactly the
baby I had imagined, a little version of myself . . . But there I
was, in a hospital gown on a Saturday morning, and my child
had Down syndrome.[3]

As a Christian, A.J. had learned the Bible verse "Be ye perfect
as your heavenly father is perfect," which—can I just say?—is a hell
of a challenge to contend with if you're a One on the Enneagram
and already lean toward perfectionism. The verse bothered A.J., so
she looked it up. As a seminary student, she had access to a Greek
dictionary and learned that the word we translate as "perfect" is
really about wholeness. Jesus meant "perfect" in the sense of "the
end for which you are created, rather than conforming to an ideal,"
A.J. said. Penny was a gift, pure and simple, perfect in the end for
which she was created.

And, just as importantly, so was A.J.

"In being given Penny, it wasn't just that I came to accept her
as someone who was both beautiful and broken, vulnerable, needy,
and gifted," she said. She also came to accept *herself* as that. Penny
and the two siblings who came along later are A.J.'s ongoing "huge
life lesson in perfectionism." Today, it's not that the anxiety is gone,
but it's tempered by a serenity that comes from having been broken
open and finding grace.

See: The One's Origin Story

The story that Ones told themselves growing up reminds me of
reading comic books.

When I was a kid, fans of superheroes fell into one of two camps: either you read DC comics focused around *The World's Finest* team of Superman and Wonder Woman or you were a die-hard Marvel fan and loved Spider-Man, Hulk, Black Widow, and assorted misfits.

As a Four, I Identified most with emotionally tortured under-dog Peter Parker (a.k.a. Spider-Man). No surprise there.

Superman, on the other hand, *bored* me. The guy had a super-power for *everything*: superspeed, supervision, superstrength, supersmarts. Writers had to work hard and rely on Superman's only weakness—Kryptonite—to come up with challenges even worthy of his powers. This issue was compounded by the fact that he's not even human.

He's an alien, an outsider who's superior to us mere mortals. Which is why, as a Four, I liked Batman, all wrapped up in all his moody, dark, brooding, self-absorbed feelings. But I digress.

I'm sure I'll catch all kinds of flak from Marvel and DC comic-book fans, but I'm sharing my recollections to make a point: *Ones work so hard to be perfect and then wonder why everyone else can't relate.* Which is ironic, of course, because they first started forming their One story in order to fit in, to please, to exceed expectations, to uphold rules and principles—all in order to get their needs met for control, esteem, and safety.

I've had several Ones share with me that when they were kids they saw a void at home or school and felt compelled to fill it. Like a superhero, they had to save their families, rescue their friends, and uphold the code of conduct they believed was right. These Ones were not only good boys and good girls but they were much more visible because they had to police others, even parents who disappointed and frustrated them when they failed to meet the Ones' high internal standards.

Some Ones were raised by parents committed to upholding impossible standards of being the best in every way imaginable. These parents often held high-profile roles as pillars of the community: prominent business owners, elected officials, family-legacy standard bearers, and civic and church leaders. They ran a tight ship in the family, or at least their One children perceived them that way. In response, the young Ones learned to contribute to the family's mission, whether that was propping up a parent's image or an aspiring career.

Or, at the other extreme, other Ones experienced a family structure that was nonexistent and loosey-goosey, with no consistent rules. In those situations, they had to become the ones reforming, redeeming, and restoring order in the home. Often a parental authority figure was missing in the household. The remaining parent battled enough of their own demons or difficulties, leaving the household in a state of flux, clutter, and chaos unless someone stepped in to establish Mary Poppins–like order.

Not every One fits into either extreme. If you read Michelle Obama's memoir, for example, you can tell she is a One who was raised by loving parents in a stable home. It's also clear, though, that she was an African American girl growing up in a racist society and that if she wanted to have any opportunities, she was going to have to be that much better than everyone else—an honor roll student at an elite high school, a student council officer, a caring daughter. My point is that there are lots of factors in a One's origin story, or in anyone's. Parents and home life play an important part in determining what story we will adopt for ourselves, but so do innate personality traits and factors of race, class, and gender.

As kids, many Ones told themselves that they would not be loved unless they met or exceeded the rules and regulations. Therefore, they learned to obey explicit as well as implicit family requisites. These kids were the well-behaved, mature-for-their-age, inherently principled natural leaders. If their family seemed too lax, then Ones crafted a story in which the responsibilities of leading and improving the household, and their family's reputation, fell to them. These Ones did the job because somebody had to—and, from their perception, no one else would or could.

Regardless of where they found themselves on the One-story spectrum, young Ones wanted to know the standards and principles of morality, decency, and integrity—and to adhere to them. These kids were often the Eagle Scouts and sports stars, the valedictorians and first-chair violinists, the scholarship winners and first-generation college graduates. They were beloved by their teachers because they acted like personal assistants in the classroom. They were usually respected by other students because they stood up to bullies, won the trophy for the team, and provided solutions.

Now, certainly, all types growing up may have fulfilled those roles as well. But, during their upbringing, Ones served in these capacities as the natural consequence of who they thought they had to be in order to avoid fault, blame, criticism, and punishment. Because Ones tell themselves a story that it's their job to make the world a better place, they're going to end up working harder, doing more, and putting in the extra hours necessary to accomplish that. And, if they weren't well-known leaders, then they were striving for other goals they considered more important: being the best Christian in church youth group, planning a career in the military, working to provide for their in-crisis family, or volunteering for a political candidate, a nonprofit, or another worthy cause.

Like Superman fighting for truth and justice, Ones are compelled to right wrongs wherever they find them. Until they discover they can't right them all, and that some of the things they assumed were wrongs are really okay the way they are. Then the One's reforming superpower becomes an unbearable burden.

Own: The Strength and Shadow of the One

Ones learn to thrive because they're always working to improve themselves and to be good. When others resent them for being too perfect, Ones point to their principles, to state laws, to the Bible, to the Constitution, to military regulations, to *The Chicago Manual of Style*, to the DSM-5, or to the requirements of basic human decency. These Ones are Good Samaritans because they couldn't live with their conscience reminding them that they walked by someone in need, which would make them bad people. Twos, on the other hand, would stop to help because they feel compelled to meet that person's needs.

We know that unconscious false beliefs in childhood keep us tangled up in our old story. We'll have a hard time living a new story if we don't see and consciously push back against these erroneous beliefs. From Ones, I've heard messages like these:

- What I *should* do is more important that what I *want* to do.
- If I don't keep my anger in check, I'll become unhinged.
- I'll finally be happy when I'm perfect.
- I need to be good so people will like me.
- I need to be right all the time.
- I have to maintain control.

- If I relax, all hell will break loose.
- The risk of being criticized or judged is not worth the shame and self-judgment it could cause.
- People will not accept me as a flawed human being.
- Others won't do as good a job as me.

These unconscious broken beliefs wreak havoc on a One's life and have nothing to do with the messages God want us to believe. Does God require perfection before we can be loved? *No.* Is grace unable to cover our mistakes? *No.* Are we supposed to maintain rigid control over our lives or surrender our will over to a higher power? *The latter.* As long as these beliefs remain unchallenged, Ones will have a hard time inhabiting the Larger Story of God.

The problem is that Ones in their old story don't make the connection that their perfectionism is the source of their unhappiness. In fact, most old-story Ones believe that their commitment to perfection is an asset rather than a liability and that their inner critic is safeguarding them from making mistakes. The story Ones repeatedly tell themselves includes self-improvement as the starting point for improving the world. Although this can take many different forms, most Ones are eager to pursue new systems, innovative practices, or fresh ideas that help them do more in order to be better. They love books and podcasts by other Ones and appreciate other leaders who share their same values and commitment to excellence. Eventually, though, whether in young adulthood or later in life, Ones hit a point where perfectionism becomes impossible and therefore undermines the whole story they have been telling themselves all along.

The compulsion to improve themselves and others becomes a problem when Ones start believing that enough is never enough. No matter how good they are, they still feel that they're not good enough. Theirs is the story of religious legalists who are committed to meritocracy, earning their goodness every day while secretly knowing it won't last. But it allows them to think they're better than others, who often don't even appear to try, let alone hit the mark.

Depending on the religious or spiritual influences when they were kids, Ones may have a strong sense of this legalistic mind-set, relying on their obedience and rule-tending as a means of becoming acceptable to their perfect, holy God. They often view the Bible as a rule manual and commandment dispenser rather than a beautiful, inspired collection of sacred scriptures featuring stories, poetry, and history. They rely on church, Bible teaching, and pastors and leaders to help them see what they must do to be good, and they are inspired by heroic stories of religious people who made great sacrifices for the sake of their faith.

As Ones grow into adulthood, many experience a near-constant voice in their head telling them to be better. I think of an example shared by one of my favorite Ones, Dr. Lee Camp, a professor of theology and ethics at Lipscomb University in Nashville and host of the amazing *Tokens Show*, a "theological variety show" carried on NPR and online. When I asked him what it was like in his shoes to be a One, Lee described how he knew he had landed on the correct type.[4] He attended an Enneagram seminar and heard the presenter say that the surefire way to know you're a One is if you have the critical voice in your head. "*What?* Doesn't everyone have that voice in their head?" Lee thought. He had experienced this critical narrator's voice in his mind for as long as he could remember. He was genuinely shocked to discover that not everyone has the same kind of critic always ready to pounce and offer harsh commentary. Growing up in a perfection-minded church, Lee provided a stunning example of how his inner critic shaped his adolescence:

> For me, it was not just a vague apprehension of punishment. It was explicitly stated if you don't do this stuff right, then you're going to go to hell. So, I remember as a sixteen-year-old driving down Alabama Highway 34 from Palo City back to my home in Talladega. I glanced down at the speedometer and I was going fifty-seven miles an hour in a fifty-five [zone]. I kid you not, the thought that went through my mind was, "Lee, you should slow down because if you were to have a car wreck and get killed going fifty-seven, you're going to go to hell." It's not worth an eternity in hell for two miles an hour. It sounds outrageous but that was my honest [assessment] . . . . That certainly has a way of screwing with your mind and your psyche, you know?

Left unchecked, this kind of scrupulosity Lee described, whether traced back to dogmatic religions, high-ground morality, or fervent patriotism, becomes toxic enough to poison all areas of a One's life. There's a right way and wrong way, and even when they face a dilemma—such as whether to speed and not break curfew or break the speed limit and risk damnation—Ones have usually prioritized or ranked their authorities.

Awaken: Counting the Cost

The cost of the story Ones tell themselves adds up quickly: simmering resentment just below the surface waiting to boil over, self-condemnation and contempt for their imperfections, and exhaustion from always striving to improve and do more. They are usually wound tight and always vigilant about what they need to do to improve everything and everyone around them. They can't bear for others to lead who don't share their values or demonstrate their commitment to integrity, but on the other hand they resent always having to make up for the lazy sods who aren't doing their part. They're tired and their old story begins to feel hopeless. Which often compels Ones to redouble their efforts at self-improvement—a good thing if it breaks them out of their stale narrative but not so good if it props up the delusion that they can work longer and try harder to be even better.

Ones who are looking to awaken to the costs of their old story should be careful of the fine line that exists between the kind of self-improvement that leads to transformation and the kind that merely polishes the acorn shell, as Cynthia Bourgeault's parable taught us in the second chapter. The good news for Ones is that they, more than any other type on the Enneagram, are fully alive to the need to be better tomorrow than they are today. That's the stuff they live for! The bad news is that they are often *not* ready for the kind of this-will-get-worse-before-it-gets-better inner work that lasting change requires of them.

I'm mindful of the way Ones are looking for ways to be better whenever I speak on the Enneagram, lead a retreat, or invite a guest on the show. I'm told more Ones and Nines listen to my *Typology* podcast than any of the other Enneagram types. This makes sense to me. Because they're in the gut triad, Ones have a complex relationship with anger. While Eights overexpress it and Nines underexpress it, Ones internalize it. If Eights externalize anger and Nines are out of touch with theirs, then Ones work hard to tamp theirs down.

Ones readily feel angry—at injustice in the world, at people who take up two parking spaces, at misplaced apostrophes in others' emails—but are committed to believing it's wrong to express that anger. In other words, a One's anger is always there, like the antique shotgun over the mantel—it shouldn't be used. Recall what A.J. told her therapist as a teenager about never getting angry. She actually believed that about herself at the time, and that kind of denial of anger is typical of Ones in an old story. Because, if they pulled the trigger, then their base instincts might take over and torch the place to the ground. And that would be bad, and that would make them bad, and they are so committed to being good that it's best just to leave anger locked up and at a distance.

But sometimes being good is no longer an option.

My wife and I have a longstanding friendship with Enneagram One Julianne Cusick. She and her husband Michael are gifted counselors, speakers, and authors. They are also founders of Restoring the Soul in Denver, Colorado. The story of their marriage and how they broke out of their respective type narratives is amazing in and of itself and crucial, I suspect, to their ability to help others change their old stories as well. Michael's struggles with sex addiction and infidelity, which he has spoken openly about in his book *Surfing for God*, took a terrible toll on their relationship.

It took Julianne years of wrestling through her despair, anger, and sorrow to experience healing in her marriage. While she chose to pursue forgiveness and restoration instead of harboring bitterness, it was a long process. As Michael left his compulsive sexual behaviors behind and repented, he won Julianne over and their marriage was restored. Many years later, however, she realized she was still struggling with resentment and anger—and that this was tied to her Oneness.

"Once our marriage was restored, I began to see how my ongoing anger and 'being right' (about almost everything!) was harming my husband and our marriage," she said.[5] "Did I want to use my justified anger over being betrayed as a weapon? For Ones, we have to accept that life is not as it should be. We operate in a world filled with unbearable disappointment and loss. To truly be free, we have to find our way in the midst of our brokenness to move toward a more hopeful future."

Rewrite: Craft Your New Story

Creating a new story requires Ones to rethink how they view the world. They have to shift paradigms, from absolutes to both/ands, from being righteous to being in relationship. The goal for Ones is to move from the Passion of anger to the Virtue of serenity, where they can let go of the need for perfection and experience wholeness and peace. When Ones have matured beyond their old script, they're remarkable—wise, powerful sages who actualize their principles in the midst of their humanity. Like Solomon faced with deciding the fate of a baby two women claimed was her own, awakened Ones refuse to adhere to the law for its own sake and instead look at the bigger picture. Solomon ordered the baby to be cut in half in a literal interpretation of the law, knowing that the child's actual mother would rather give up her right to him than see him harmed.

Part of serenity is seeing the good in life. Ones breaking out of their old story practice *agere contra* by making R and R a priority, scheduling vacations, days off, and downtime in order to recharge. They laugh and cut loose, start the conga line, and don't worry about what everyone else is thinking. As my friend Richard Rohr—himself a One—says, one of the "lifetime tasks" of Ones is "to learn occasionally to ignore duty, order, and the improvement of the world, and instead to play, celebrate, and enjoy life."[6] In the Enneagram arrow system, Ones "go to Seven" in security, meaning that in times of health they can happily embody the freedom and *joie de vivre* that define Sevens. Ones in a new story accept themselves just as they are, knowing that imperfection is essential. They forgive themselves when they fall short and move on without beating themselves up.

Richard has also learned the wisdom of consciously leaning into his Nine wing. As harmonizers, "Nines don't need to be right like we Ones do," he says.[7] "It's my salvation." Sometimes, he will get away from the hustle of his life as a priest and a spiritual leader to go on a long retreat, including a forty-day hermitage retreat he took at the Abbey of Gethsemani, living in the little hut Thomas Merton once occupied. During the retreat, he says, "I could stop saving the world, making recordings, preaching all around the world. I could turn off that whole Two motor that I had to help, help, help everybody, save everybody." When Ones lean into their Nine wing, they can enjoy the gift of the Nine, which is peace.

Ones in a new groove are admired for their integrity, reliability, and fairmindedness. They're known for pitching in and improving anything that needs their help, but they're also comfortable letting things be, allowing others to figure out their own means and methods. That's serenity. These maturing Ones don't mind the tension of ambiguity and uncertainty. They trust that upholding truth, whatever that may look like, is not their job alone. They can endure clutter, disorder, and chaos without running around correcting others and modeling the right way to do things. Evolved Ones realize that they have more to offer than just quick fixes and logical solutions. Instead they take to heart the wisdom of Anne Lamott: "Lighthouses don't go running all over an island looking for boats to save; they just stand there shining."[8]

In order to break out of their legalistic mind-set, healthy Ones practice the spiritual discipline of stillness and Sabbath rest. For many, it's challenging to get out of the always-in-motion mind-set and behaviors of their old story but more than worth it to achieve more equilibrium. Because as they soften their grip on perfection, they discover opportunities for holding someone's hand, for receiving what Brené Brown calls the "gifts of imperfection."[9] In her book, Brown offers a number of suggestions for perfectionists as they seek to live in a new story. Some of those are what you might expect, but others are refreshing, like letting go of what other people think, letting go of the need for certainty, and letting go of exhaustion as a status symbol. (Are you listening, overworked Ones?) She also talks about the freedom that perfectionists often feel when they muster up the courage to admit their imperfections and mistakes to others. Rather than encountering the condemnation they feared—often, the condemnation they've been heaping on themselves all along—they've found compassion from others who have also been there. Voicing their vulnerabilities and mistakes out loud is a critical spiritual practice for Ones who are moving from anger to serenity. They find that the world doesn't end just because they failed to hold it up.

And in that realization lies the path to freedom.

Ideas for the One's New Story

Serenity doesn't happen overnight. Rather, it's the product of many small choices and decisions that Ones can make to embrace *agere contra*. The "do the opposite of what you would normally do" advice is spot on for Ones, but they should start modestly rather than thinking they'll change their ways overnight.

Here's a small change: Choose one drawer, shelf, or corner of your desk to keep cluttered and unorganized as a reminder that you don't have to control your environment in order to be happy. If you're feeling really ambitious, buy a husky and let it shed on your furniture. Breathe. Mess with your schedule too. Call in sick to work (whoa, pushing limits) to relax and go somewhere you normally wouldn't go: an afternoon matinee, an unsanitary water park, an exhibition of steamy Robert Mapplethorpe photos. But I jest.

To get a handle on the constant self-critical commentary running through your mind, give your inner critic a persona, a name, and physical description—especially one that's exaggerated, funny, or a caricature. My editor, who is a One, has named her judgmental inner voice Aunt Gertrude and pictures her as the Church Lady that comedian Dana Carvey used to play on *Saturday Night Live*. When she catches herself in a spiral of negative self-judgment, she mentally thanks Aunt Gertrude for weighing in and then invites her to take a long walk off a short pier. So, start telling Sister Mary

Severity, Sir Nigel, Aunt Millicent, Drill Sergeant Sam, or whatever you decide to name your critic to be quiet when you recognize their refrain echoing in your mind. Let them know they can have a voice and ride on your bus but, as Elizabeth Gilbert says, they're not allowed to drive or even touch the map.[10]

It sounds corny, but look in the mirror each morning and say, "I'm going to risk making some big-ass mistakes today, and don't try to stop me." And then determine that you're going to extend this same grace to other people. Instead of criticizing someone who makes a mistake, applaud them for trying. Practice authentic compassion by figuring out how to encourage them. Notice what it feels like to stop judging others who don't meet your standards of excellence. Trust me, it's sweet relief not to have to police the world.

As a type Four, I find security in borrowing the One's habits of self-discipline, hard work, and upholding what I believe in. I'm inspired by Ones like my friend Richard Rohr and humanitarian leaders like former President Jimmy Carter. Ones who break out of their type-rutted story radiate with the kind of charisma, integrity, and good-heartedness that attract others without effort. They shine with a kind of idealism that has substance without the brittle veneer of perfectionism. These beautiful Ones accept others, warts and all, without judgment, just as they accept themselves.

When Ones really get it that they no longer have to be perfect, they can become serene participants in that Larger Story that always ends well.

6

The Two's Story

Self-Care for the Helper

*"As you grow older you will discover that
you have two hands. One for helping
yourself, the other for helping others."*
—Audrey Hepburn

Al Andrews had been waiting for weeks to see his favorite scene
from one of his favorite movies. This was decades ago, when
he was in his twenties. Back in the day before our favorite movies
and shows were available 24/7, you sat glued to the set or you
would miss it entirely. And he definitely did not want to miss it.
It's that scene from *The Miracle Worker* where the blind, deaf, and
nonverbal girl Helen Keller *finally* begins to understand that, when
her teacher pours water again and again over her hand while spell-
ing out W-A-T-E-R in her palm with sign language letters, the two
things are connected.

"It's just the most beautiful scene in any movie," Al told me with awe in his voice.[1] Since Al is a Two on the Enneagram, it didn't surprise me at all that the movie he loved so much, that he would work his entire schedule around watching, was about a woman who drops everything in her life to save a girl everyone else had given up on. It figures. Twos are like that.

Al was pumped to see that tear-jerker scene again. And then the phone rang.

"Of course, I answered it, because it's very responsible and helpful to answer the phone," he said. Since Caller ID didn't exist back in those dark old days before Netflix on demand, he couldn't see in advance who it was and make a judgment about whether it was important enough to answer right then or call them back later. So, he picked up the phone, because that's the kind of thing Helpers do.

It was a perfectly ordinary call—not an emergency, just a friend checking in—so it would have been fine for him to say, "Hey, can I call you back in half an hour? I'm doing something right now." But that's not what Al did.

Instead, he stayed on the line, polite and helpful on the outside but quietly seething. "Internally I raged," he said. "I was just mad at this person and they didn't do anything wrong." He did not express any irritation at all because that might hurt the caller's feelings and he didn't want to disappoint.

Al spent the decade of his twenties like that, he remembers: doing whatever he thought needed to be done in order to serve others, no matter what he wanted for himself. "I spent my time looking around to see where I could be of help. I was just the most helpful friend you could ever have. I would show up if you needed me to help you move, even if my back was hurting."

Part of him realized even at the time that he was doing all this to win people's approval and that being a perpetual Giving Tree was probably not a healthy dynamic. "It fed me knowing they would think well of me and would perhaps like me more," he admitted. "And I would keep my reputation as a super helper."

But his constant giving was taking a serious toll. He was exhausted and depressed, and by his early thirties he realized he needed help.

He realized he needed help. It sounds so easy, right? But not necessarily for Twos, because their fundamental identity is that *they* are the helpers, and helpers do not need help.

So, the breakthrough for Al, the watershed moment when he began to recognize that the story he'd been living in all along wasn't working, came not just in the insights from a seasoned professional counselor. It happened before that, in the decision to see a therapist at all. "That was the start of the shift, I think," he said—simply admitting he was a person with needs and that, if he constantly disavowed them, he would lose himself. "Others' needs were always in front of mine. In my heart, that was not a noble thing, but a necessary thing. I didn't think about my own needs."

Al had allowed his self-worth to become wrapped up in a story that told him he was only worthy of love and relationship if he was meeting the needs of others. When he started challenging that story, he began to grow.

See: The Two's Origin Story

Like other members of Al's always-helpful tribe of Twos, he formed a story early in life that provided a way for him to survive and win the love of others. Twos don't have to grow up in unstable or difficult circumstances to internalize the message that they must take care of others; Al reports that he "grew up in a lovely family" with parents who cared well for him and his sister. Still, even in that safe and loving situation Al internalized the message that his main job was to stay positive and help others. "In our family there was one primary acceptable emotion, and that was happy. We're going to be happy. And so we were." When challenges or sad events happened, the family reframed them. If the dog died, they'd get another dog right away. That was the message.

Al came to believe that if he discussed any of the things that made him sad or distressed, it would only "make everybody uncomfortable and pull them away from the happy. So, I just kind of pushed those down."

Simply put, there was little room for Al's needs in his family, which is the case for many Helper Twos I know. The road to receiving the love, affirmation, and security every child needs became for Twos a matter of pleasing and giving. They started weaving a story around the false belief that they were not allowed to have or express their own needs. To do so would be considered selfish, and a shameful rejection of the family rules.

What are the unconscious and misguided beliefs that follow Twos into adulthood and glue their old story in place? Al mentioned some of them, but here are a few more.

- My needs are so great, they will overpower anyone who sees them.
- People like people who are always cheery and who flatter them.
- People who know me should already know what I need.
- If I express my needs, others will reject and abandon me.

- I probably want too much.
- Winning the approval of others is key to my feeling worthy.
- I should always try to please others, even if I make myself miserable in the process.
- It's a give-to-get world.
- I am either indispensable or worthless.
- I'm powerful only when I'm giving, not receiving.
- I'm nobody if nobody likes me.

As with all the types, the sooner Twos bring these toxic beliefs into conscious awareness and replace them with healthy ones, the sooner they can get on with living into a truer, better story.

Young Twos learn to disown their needs and focus on helping those around them. Like other types highly attuned to their surroundings, Twos sense the moods of others and find a way to meet their needs—materially, emotionally, physically, financially, or in whatever way they can. Because this behavior can resemble what Nines do, Twos and Nines are one of the most common mistypes on the Enneagram. They both want to please people and intuit in advance what they want. But they do it for different reasons: Nines are adapting in order to avoid conflict and Twos are adjusting their image to make you like them. And, with what they give others, Twos automatically expect to have their own unexpressed needs met in return.

Al calls this expectation the result of his "inner conniver." Back in his unevolved days before he came to recognize the default patterns of his old story, he would unconsciously attach strings to the help he gave to others. Other Twos I've known confirm this transactional story formation. One of my favorite Enneagram teachers,

Beatrice Chestnut, a past president of the International Enneagram Association and author of the classic book *The Complete Enneagram: 27 Paths to Greater Self-Knowledge*, described it as "strategic giving." Although such giving may be unconscious, especially at first, it boils down to "If I take care of you, then you'll take care of me."[2]

As a Two, Beatrice is keenly aware of how her type learned to fashion a functional story in order to get their needs met. "One of the things I like about the Enneagram," she said, "is the way it's based on where our attention goes. Whatever we're paying attention to gets a lot of energy from us." This is true of all the types, of course, but as part of the feeling-based heart triad, Twos focus on relationships, specifically, how their relating to others fills their own need for love and esteem.

Beatrice explained, "For me, I'm always focused on other people: How are other people feeling? What's the status of our connection? Are we in a good rapport, are people liking what I'm doing? Things like that. A lot of my focus is around how to improve or create a positive rapport with other people, especially important people." Her hope is always that, if she supports them, they will support her in reciprocal fashion.

As they grow up, Twos also begin to gravitate toward meeting the needs of others in ways that reflect their own. They're the best friends who listen and console others' broken hearts. They're the gift-givers and party-throwers, quick wits with a well-timed joke to lift the mood or shift the tone of a group. They offer rides, deliver meals, pet sit for neighbors, shovel snow-covered driveways for the elderly, and raise money for worthy causes. Two children have a knack for befriending misfits and cheering the lonely. They intuit what the adults around them need and provide whatever they can—helping with chores and sometimes even providing a small shoulder for grownups to cry on.

Like the stories other types tell themselves, this one works—until it doesn't.

Own: The Strength and Shadow of the Two

Twos, Threes, and Fours form the heart triad, focused on feelings. These three types each create a variation on the theme that they cannot be loved for who they really are; therefore, they create a story-persona that allows them to mask their true self and what they believe are its deficiencies and instead fill the role they assume will go over well with those around them. While Threes adopt the role of the successful achiever and Fours become special and unique, Twos become the Helpers. They cultivate an upbeat, positive persona eager to lend a hand, bring a bouquet, loan the money, host the event, mourn another's loss, and give more than anyone else.

Such compassion and generosity may have enabled Twos to endure what was an otherwise unbearable situation. Some were deprived of attention, affection, and affirmation, building blocks of healthy self-esteem in children. With no other way to get their natural needs met, Twos found a way to make a meal for themselves from the crumbs of others' gratitude. They wanted love and settled for appreciation. As adults, however, they continue to starve without realizing that they have the power finally to change their story—to ask others directly for what they need and to practice healthy self-care.

The false story Twos tell themselves is that being open about their own needs will only reveal their unlovable true selves, leading to humiliation and rejection, so they work at being indispensable to those around them. They make their homes inviting and encourage others to drop by unannounced. They're always willing to offer a sofa to sleep on and gas money for those struggling to get by. They make great counselors, teachers, mentors, nonprofit activists, and community volunteers. (You will not be surprised to learn that Al became a professional therapist.)

Advice is given thoughtfully and dispensed liberally by Twos, who often share solutions with others who haven't asked for help or prefer to solve their own problems. Undeterred by polite resistance, they give out their number and encourage others to call them day or night. No matter someone else's problem, Twos will find a way to fix it. As a Two friend once told me, "If all my friends jumped off a bridge, I wouldn't follow. I'd be at the bottom to catch them when they fall!"

Twos listen carefully and hear the needs expressed by others even when others might not be aware of what they're revealing. They're accustomed to using such focused, unbridled generosity to ingratiate themselves into others' lives.

And, I'm sure, many times it probably works. Instead of building relationships on shared interests, earned trust, and experiences over time, Twos buy into their old story and assume no one would like or want them just for who they are. They mistakenly believe that, if they stopped helping, giving, and serving, then others would abandon them. So, they continue ingratiating themselves in ways that are, paradoxically, often generous and disingenuous at the same time.

When their gifts or offers of assistance are rejected or politely declined, they sometimes act deeply offended. "I was just trying to help," Twos often say, followed by, "Forgive me for caring and trying to do the right thing." Such a response frequently elicits a reluctant willingness from others to accept their help after all. Twos are determined to get their foot in the door until the door opens and they're invited in.

In fact, at times, Twos are downright relentless about finding people to need them. While their caregiving is often universal and indiscriminate, Twos frequently notice easy marks who are weaker, needier, and less capable. Providing what they perceive such individuals need, Twos unconsciously consider these people indebted to them even though they usually try to act like there are no strings attached. Which can be confusing and frustrating to those being served. Twos are saying, "No, you don't need to pay me back—please, I wouldn't dream of it! This is my gift to you," while unconsciously thinking, "I wonder if they'll meet my needs in the future without my having to ask for it directly."

When others don't reciprocate or show what Twos consider adequate appreciation, then Helpers slide into extremes—either as the wounded martyr whose saintly deeds go unnoticed or as the desperate stalker attempting to do even more for those in their sights. The people they want to help understandably end up creating distance or establishing boundaries, preventing Twos from getting the affirmation they believe must come from others. Those in relationship with Twos may even pity them for being so clingy and desperate to be part of others' lives. Depending on their own type-stories, others may jump in and try to rescue Twos in distress, once again meeting Twos' needs indirectly. When Twos *don't* get what they think they need from others, they tap into the sore spots of their past, often experiencing overwhelming waves of cumulative fear, grief, and anger.

Once Twos realize their usual methods are driving others away, they judge anyone who withdraws from them as ungrateful and unworthy. They reinforce their story by creating walls and acting as if they don't need anything from others. You can bet the ranch, though, that most Twos immediately begin looking for other, more deserving, targets of their lavish attention.

Like all types caught by the undertow of their story, Twos keep swimming in circles. Until they realize the cost of fighting the current, they can't grab the lifeline that's right in front of them.

Awaken: Counting the Cost

Twos have so many wonderful, positive, nurturing gifts to give the rest of us. But, if they're unwilling to unmask their counterfeit story, they're never going to discover a new story to live.

It often takes a relational crisis of some kind for Twos to awaken to the story they've been living and to make changes in how they move forward. For Lisa-Jo Baker, the author of books like *Never Unfriended* (you can't make that up) and *Surprised by Motherhood*, it was that she began in middle age to understand the unhealthy dynamics she was enabling as a Two and how much she resented all the time and energy she was expending on serving people.[3] As a child, she had stepped into the role of family helper after her mother died, acting as the intermediary between her father's anger and her siblings' needs.

Even when she was twenty years old, she was still called upon to be the "hostage negotiator" on international calls with her father and new stepmother, who were arguing with each other. So, even though she was an adult and even though she lived in another country at the time, it was still her job to calm her father down.

It took her many years to be able to say, "This is not my job anymore." Part of what changed was that she had become a mother herself and learned to set some boundaries with her own kids, who were, like all children, "bottomless holes of need." At the end of a day of driving them around and helping with homework and preparing their meals, all she wanted was a chance to sit on the sofa and relax. But the kids would keep needing things from her.

"I don't understand why you can't just go watch a show," her husband said.

"I don't understand how you *can*," Lisa-Jo replied. "Don't you feel guilty? Don't you feel like these kids still need something from us?"

"No. I don't." He was puzzled. He did not have a problem with going "off duty" at the end of the day, which made Lisa wonder: What would that be like?

One thing she found helpful was when he said out loud, "Listen to me. You have permission! Go and rest." She knows in her mind that she doesn't need another person to give her permission to take breaks, but hearing it helps to interrupt the circuit of her old story—the one that says her worth is wrapped up in other people's happiness and that she's only valuable insofar as she is meeting their needs.

So, Lisa-Jo began discovering the freedom that came with setting boundaries with her children. "Your feelings are not the boss of me," she tells them now—and she means it.

She has also taken another huge step in setting boundaries in her relationship with her father. Once when she was visiting him, she disagreed about something he had said, and he was shocked.

"I tried to disagree politely, but the more I disagreed, the more he just . . . he pointed his finger in my face and said, 'Stop it. No. Stop it. You stop saying that to me.'" Lisa-Jo is quick to point out that her father has had his own journey of transformation since then, but at the time, he was deeply threatened by even this simple example of Lisa-Jo's standing up for herself and having her own opinion.

I want to note that, for each of the nine types, the Awaken step is difficult, as it asks you to become aware of your default script in real time and take actions to change it. But I think this is particularly difficult for Twos, who are so keyed in to pleasing others. So, let's get this out there right now: your awakening is *not* going to please everyone around you. You're going to piss off some people. Many people, like Lisa-Jo's father, will have gotten comfortable with the way you've always bent over backwards to put their needs ahead of your own. They will be confused by your decision to set boundaries and to separate your happiness from theirs. But, take it from Lisa-Jo and countless other Twos who have made this leap, you'll find freedom on the other side.

Rewrite: Craft Your New Story

Lisa-Jo's transformation has been a joy to behold. That's also true of Al. Remember that back in his twenties he was outwardly giving even while resentment built up inside him. As I said, a breakthrough happened when he decided to seek therapy. Another happened when he became a therapist himself. In those early years, Al "would take it home"—all of his clients' suffering, all their pain. "I would feel it. I would bear a huge weight on me," he said.

His mentor took him aside and offered some perspective. "Al, people are very resilient," the more experienced therapist advised. "Often, the people that you're helping have been dealing with this thing for fifteen, twenty, even thirty years. They'll make it until next week."

That was an epiphany for Al. His job was not to save people in one dramatic act, but to understand that he was just one piece of their journey. "I'm not the final answer here," he realized. Other people would also help his clients. God was at work in their lives. Heck, his clients might even find relief and insight from seeing the right bumper sticker at the right time. He was just one part of the process.

Al's hard-won humility pushes back against the Two's old story, which is that their help is indispensable. The Enneagram Passion for Twos may sound surprising: it's pride. That doesn't mean they're puffed up about their achievements (although some of them are) or that they think they're always right about everything. For Twos, pride manifests in an inability to admit their own neediness. As Enneagram author Alice Fryling explains, "They may be proud of the fact that they know what you need, but you do not know what they need."[4] There is a "where would the world be without me?" nature to the pride of a Two. They don't admit that they have needs like other people.

In order to redirect their old story, Twos can develop the ability to regularly hit pause so that new choices can replace default habits. As Beatrice Chestnut shared, revising her story as a Two requires patience: "When I was first working on myself, I made my mantra: *What do I need right now?* What do I really need in this moment? Answering that question required a lot of compassion, self-compassion, and no judgment. I realized it was okay not to know at first. I could allow 'I don't know' to be a legitimate answer. Getting in touch with needs and also getting in touch with your own sense of self is really important for Twos."

What lies at the other side of this process is the Virtue of the Two: humility. This means finally accepting that they don't have all the time, treasure, and insight to help everyone. It also means that Twos recognize that their needs are as important as everyone else's. Just as there is freedom for Ones in admitting their mistakes to others, there is freedom for Twos in admitting their neediness. That they are often lonely, sad, and *human*, just like everybody else. Special but not special. When Twos can own their needs, they're beginning to rewrite their story.

That's how Al has become one of the most evolved Twos I know. Where I live in Nashville, he is a bit of a legend because of a service he founded called Porter's Call, which provides free counseling to musicians and recording artists. I can't tell you how many people I've heard say to me, "I went through a period of my life that was horrible, and Al Andrews helped put me back together."

But Al has healthy boundaries now. He's no longer someone who *must* help, as an unhealthy Two is and as he once was. He is someone who often chooses to be *available* to help.

Ideas for the Two's New Story

New-story Twos stop focusing exclusively on how to help others in order to explore how to meet their own needs. Asking for what they need directly is crucial. As is resisting the default tendency to soothe, nurture, fix, assist, and connect with everyone they meet.

If you're a Two, transformation needs to start from within you, so *agere contra* means paying attention to your own needs. You're already too wrapped up in other people and their feelings as it is. Instead, become a detective and investigate your *own* motives, expectations, and emotions. Take note of your emotional status three or four times a day, jotting it in your phone or in a notebook. There are also apps you can use for this purpose, such as MoodKit and Daylio. Whatever method you use, pay attention to how you feel and not just what you're intuiting about the emotional states of those around you.

Make a list of your top ten current needs right now—whether physical, emotional, financial, or spiritual. Think about a specific task you know you need help with but have resisted asking for it. Now think of three people who would be glad to help you with this task. Ask until one agrees. Then make it a point *not* to do anything special for that person between now and when they come help you. In fact, other than a sincere "thank you," don't give them anything afterward. Also, don't pick up a little gift for them when you're at the grocery store.

Remember that part of the transformation that comes with changing your old Two story is humbly asking for the help that you need. In fact, going forward, make asking directly for what you need a habit you practice every day. As you write down your moods and feelings, keep a log of that too: What did you ask for today, and from whom? What happened?

If you're like many other Twos, you may have a subconscious balance sheet you're carrying around in your head, a litany of past favors you've done and the debts incurred for them. Spend some time reflecting, journaling, and listing all the old unconscious grudges you may still harbor and unpaid debts others owe you. Be honest about how you feel and don't hold back. Don't be freaked out if you're much angrier than you knew. Think about why you're so angry in each case. Also, don't be surprised if you have a long list of people who owe you money or have taken advantage of your generosity and time. When you clung to your false story that said you needed other people to need you in order to have any worth, you probably encouraged a number of relationships that lacked healthy boundaries. Take a breath and remember that you're starting something new.

When you finish the grudge-and-debt inventory, try to slowly resolve each item you listed. If some are minor and you can let them go, then do it. If others require a conversation to express your feelings and clear the air, schedule it—preferably in person. If debts can be written off, do it and let the debtor know. If not, let them know you'd like to discuss a system for them to repay what they owe you. In all cases, do what must be done to forgive others. Then forgive yourself for resenting and begrudging them for so long.

As you move forward in your new story, stay vigilant about how often you find yourself sniffing out other people's needs. Practice paying attention to how often your impulse to help someone kicks in—especially with people you don't know well or at all. Don't be shocked if it's a component to every encounter you have with other people most days. As you grow more aware of your default tendency to help, try to create space instead of immediately jumping in to lend a hand or offer a compliment. This might look like counting to ten in some instances and walking away from a situation in others. Try saying no to someone every day. As you practice this, you'll begin to realize which things you truly *do* want to do—the projects and people you feel genuinely called to help. And it will become easier to maintain boundaries for the other things.

Our world would be a sadder, lonelier, needier place without the vibrant gifts Twos offer. Think of all the nurses, doctors, counselors, pastors, priests, nuns, teachers, nonprofit founders, fundraisers, good neighbors, and great friends who are Twos.

It may sound cheesy, but I love the new-story mantra shared by a friend of mine: "It's okay for a Two to become number one." He's right—it's not only *okay* but it's *essential*.

Twos are never second best when they put their needs first.

7

The Three's Story

Pause for the Performer

*"Forget about being impressive and commit to
being real. Because being real is impressive!"*
—Jonathan Harnisch

My friend Lisa Whelchel's earliest memory is one of performing. She was three years old and her mom had signed her
up for a nursery rhyme reciting class with other children. Each
child was supposed to learn one nursery rhyme over six weeks to
recite in front of their families at the end of the summer.

But Lisa kicked it up a notch.

"I memorized *all* the nursery rhymes, plus I added hand motions
and choreography, all with this really big smile on my face," she
once shared with me.[1] Her teacher had her go last and be the grand
finale. When she finished performing, there was tremendous
applause, including from the people she most wanted to impress:

her parents. "I remember catching my father's eye in the back and having this sense, 'I think he likes me.'" Her mother was also delighted, picking Lisa up and proudly carrying her around as they greeted the other parents.

"In that moment the message I got was, 'Don't just do what's expected of you—do more than what's expected. If you do it really big, then you will have the love and acceptance everyone craves.'"

That's the message she carried with her when she started school, becoming a straight-A student and the teacher's pet. It's what she internalized when she became a Christian at age ten and was determined "to be the best Christian ever." And it was what pushed her to achieve when she started acting in childhood. "I got everything I ever auditioned for," she said, moving from local roles to a coveted slot on *The New Mickey Mouse Club* at age twelve.

Lisa was actually the one who made that audition happen—Disney had already done a nationwide talent search but hadn't come to the Dallas area, where she lived. So, plucky Lisa wrote a letter and said her father would pay to fly her to Los Angeles if they would only give her a chance to audition. She got the part, beating out a young Courtney Love in the process.[2]

That kind of drive landed Lisa other roles as a teenager, including her big break as the preppy Blair Warner on *The Facts of Life*, a hit sitcom that ran for nine years. Her need for success, she told me, "just went on and on and on—it really has been the script of my life."

When the show ended, Lisa was ready for the next successful stage of her life, becoming a pastor's wife and a mother. "We filmed the last episode of *The Facts of Life* in March of 1988. I got married in July of '88. I got pregnant in '89 and then I had a

child in 1990, '91, and '92. So, I even do childbirth as a Three."
She homeschooled her kids and was known for her organization,
breaking their schedules down into fifteen-minute increments for
snack time, craft time, and the like. "I was a very efficient mother,"
she said. "I wanted them to have the best childhood ever and I
wanted to be the best mother ever." She also racked up further accomplishments, publishing books and, when her kids were grown,
becoming a fan favorite on *Survivor.*

Lisa's a particularly high-profile example, but her desire to win
the admiration of others is characteristic of type Three, aptly named
the Performer. Early in life, Threes conform to the expectations
of the important people in their lives—expectations that reflect
favorably on themselves, their families, and even their religious
traditions. Notice the way Lisa said she wanted to be at the top of
her game at all times as an actor, as a mother, and as a person of faith.
That's the pressure Threes put on themselves at a very early age. As
they grow up, they often abandon vital pieces of their true self, unconsciously believing they have to disown certain parts of themselves
in order to be loved.

Lisa has spent a great deal of time over the years learning about
personality and the Enneagram, so she's familiar with many of the
darker aspects of being a Three, like being personable to everyone but personal with very few. A turning point for her was when
she realized well into adulthood that she didn't have a best friend.
Threes are easy to like, especially since they work hard to make
you like and admire them. But they can also be guarded, careful
to present themselves in ways that are most flattering. Lisa, as an
evolved Three, knows she's heading into a danger zone whenever
she finds herself rehearsing ahead of time what she's going to say to

someone else in order to get affirmation. And she knows she's liable to "amplify" or exaggerate the truth to make herself look good, though her religious convictions have kept her from sculpting the truth, which can be a problem with unevolved Threes.

"I can read a room and I can read people's feelings," Lisa said. "That's a good thing, but it can also be a negative thing if it causes me to adjust my authentic self based on my fear of their rejection or perception."

That's an excellent summary of the shadow side of Threes, whose authenticity can be lost in their drive to climb another rung on the ladder of success.

See: The Three's Origin Story

Similar to their heart-triad counterparts, Twos and Fours, the origin story of Threes revolves around their central belief cemented early in life: they can't be loved simply for who they are.

While Twos became worthy by meeting the needs of others and Fours did it by being special and unique, young Threes learned that achievements and trophies got them enough validation and affirmation to get by. The important people in their lives, overtly or unintentionally, often didn't value little Threes for who they were but only for what they achieved. These parents were not necessarily neglectful or disengaged from their children's lives; on the contrary, many Threes indicate that they felt especially close to one particular parent, often the same-gender parent but not always, who instilled in them a sense of ambition. This led to their feeling valued.

Many times, these parental figures aren't aware of how they are conditioning their kids to become so performance-driven. In some cases, they're trying to ignite the drive to win that their own parents kindled before them. They're trying to break the records and claim the accolades they were denied or else to continue the legacy of a high-achieving family. The message their children hear is that they have to be successful in order to be loved. And, for some, this leads to a pattern in which the "success = love" bar is raised higher and higher. They say, "Well, since that last award got me love, if I really double down, I'm going to get a *lot* of love."

Growing up, young Threes may have been born into a role already weighted with such lofty expectations that they never realized the pressure on them until adulthood. Some describe growing up in families in which they were not just expected to achieve but to follow one particular path that had been laid down by their parents: that they had to become a doctor, for example, or attend a particular school. The sense Threes get from this is that their own dreams don't matter; they have to do whatever it takes to meet the family's expectations.

As a result of being the family star or hero, young Threes learn to excel in any and every environment. They have to be smarter, stronger, faster, and more prepared than anyone else. Fueled by the desire to please such a demanding audience and to avoid the shame and anger associated with whatever constituted losing, these Threes didn't stop until they were on top. Their pattern of success became their identity.

I think about another friend I've had on the show, Jeff Goins. As you'd expect from any good Three, Jeff is an award-winning blogger, sought-after speaker, and bestselling author of multiple books. He teaches online courses, and he's pretty sure he makes the world's best guacamole. But, amidst all his accomplishments, he realized one day that he still didn't know if he had pleased his father. Jeff explained, "Not too long ago, I had a conversation with my dad and I got really frustrated. And I said, 'Gosh, Dad. *What do I need to do to make you proud of me?*'"[3]

While everyone wants parental approval at some level, Threes want it but don't always realize it when they get it. Jeff went on to tell his father, "I've never asked you for money. I've never needed anything from you. I went out and paid for college through grants and scholarships, and working during the summer. Even when things were tight, I figured it out. I didn't have sex before marriage; I didn't knock anybody up." While he wasn't perfect, he always had a strong moral compass and tried to do the right thing. And he racked up impressive accomplishments at work over the years, becoming a bestselling author, starting his own business, and staying out of debt. So, when Jeff enumerated all this, his dad was sort of taken aback and said, "Nothing. I'm proud of everything you've done." Jeff hadn't known that until that moment.

Unconscious mistaken beliefs and perceptions rule our lives and perpetuate the falsity of our old story. They have to be exposed for what they are—lies. I'm not sure if Jeff would say he signed on to this list of beliefs, but many Threes tell me they identified with them until they woke up and began to disentangle themselves from them.

- I'd be happier if I were more successful.
- If I'm not number one, I'm nothing.
- The world rewards doing, not being.
- I'm valuable when others admire me.
- Failure isn't an option.

- Image and appearance matter a lot.
- If you're not a somebody, you're nobody.
- It's okay to wear a mask to win over different types of people.

It's vital to see that the childhood story and the Three's false beliefs are in conflict with the gospel. Being does matter more than doing. Surface is not as important as substance. Failure does not get the last word. It is not okay to project a false self. And success does not equal happiness. If they want to be free to live in a new story, Threes must let go of these beliefs.

Own: The Strength and Shadow of the Three

Threes use their strengths not to survive but to *thrive*. Of all the types, Threes often appear to be the most confident, laser-focused, and put-together. Depending on the audience for whom they're performing, they usually make winning look easy, effortless. Keep in mind, though, that their strength is performing and adapting to whatever will please and impress the crowd.

Image-conscious and savvy, Threes are able to pivot instantly and be charming, earnest, personable, accessible, and identifiable—whatever it takes to win over an investor, convince a jury, entertain guests, defeat an opponent, or inspire a crowd. Threes are the ultimate method actors, anticipating what a particular individual, group, or audience wants from them and then, as Lisa mentioned, giving them more than what's expected. No wonder so many superstar entertainers are powerhouse Threes.

Threes survive by taking charge and leading, expecting others to work as hard and sacrifice as much as they do in order to hit targets and bring goals to life. They're organized, efficient, and capable and almost always have multiple plans in progress at any given time. Following through comes naturally to most Threes as long as the means lead to a payoff—earning the degree, launching the start-up, winning the championship, getting the corner office, exceeding a million followers on Instagram. Highly competitive in almost all arenas, Threes learn to identify what's required to beat their opponents and win the game.

And they do all this with dazzle and charm. While Nines, the Peacemakers, understand and appreciate various points of view in a conflict, therefore seeing a win-win way forward, Threes are relentless about getting what they want for themselves or their organizations. This doggedness is also true of Sevens and Eights, who join Threes in what the Enneagram calls the "aggressive stance": they see what they want and they just go and get it. Faced with an obstacle or inconvenience, Threes hammer away at what they want while often offering some kind of consolation prize or perceived conciliatory gesture to other stakeholders.

While adept at finding solutions that benefit them, Threes don't often know how to handle the emotional responses of others. They're not sure how to respond to others' feelings because they're so out of touch with their own. Which brings us to their shadow side and the steep price of their success: because they are so singularly focused on appearing successful, Threes lose touch with their emotions and other facets of identity that lead to their true self.

Threes define themselves by their resumés. They become overidentified with what they do and tend to equate their worth with their accomplishments. Without all that achievement to impress other people, they fear they are nothing at all. As Jeff Goins told me, "Other people's perception of me in some ways defines my own perception of myself." If he gave his old story a name, it could be titled *I Must Be a Success Because You Think So*. Like most Threes, his weakness emerges when he can't win the approval of others or their standards seem to shift.

Many Threes can't fathom that others would reject what they do—especially if they're knocking it out of the park—and instead want them for who they are. Threes who are stuck in an old story don't have an awareness of an identity, a true self, beyond what they do, so it's often confusing and even terrifying when others call them out or glimpse more of who they truly are. They're much more comfortable sticking to their old script—it's worked before, so why change it?—than risking the unfamiliar, uncomfortable vulnerability and transparency required for a new one. Threes are notorious workaholics, priding themselves on eighty-hour work weeks, on responding to texts and emails during the weekend, on being prepared ahead of everyone else. They struggle with work-life balance like no other type and almost always feel "on," instantly switching into work mode since they never really shut down. Threes tell themselves that anything less than hyperproductivity is second best, lazy, and a precursor to failure. This story has created such a rut in their psyches that when they try to change their habits without changing their story, Threes promptly fall off the wagon. They feel like they simply cannot help themselves—they believe they have to work because they have little sense of who they are apart from what they do.

Consequently, Threes can be incredibly resistant to any attempts to change their behavior and focus on the emotional, the spiritual, and the psychological. When pressed on internal change or required by others to reveal themselves, Threes may grow insecure and retreat into denial and incredulity.

Perhaps the most image-conscious of all Enneagram types, Threes may also channel their frustration into vanity and narcissism, clinging to the belief that others must never see 'em sweat, that they must always be dressed for success, well-groomed and ready to go into action. Threes know how to look the part no matter what's going on around them. *Fake it 'til you make it* was the message graffitied in the minds of all up-and-coming Performers. They may work out routinely if not obsessively to maintain the level of fitness they deem necessary to look their best. Some are also willing to rely on stimulants like caffeine and even performance-enhancing drugs to stay diligently focused.

A Three's motto is often *Whatever it takes*.

But what it takes is a massive toll on their bodies, their relationships, and their souls.

Awaken: Counting the Cost

Most Threes don't begin the process of counting the cost and changing their old story until the fault lines beneath their carefully landscaped lawns give way to a massive quake. They often remain asleep in their treadmill patterns longer than other types for the same two reasons that tent-pole their broken stories: they're successful and they can't bear to admit the truth if they're not. "Why would I want to do any kind of inner work if my outer life is working for me?" they ask. After all, they *look* good, and that's what they've always valued.

Threes may continue acting out their old story longer than people of other types. Many Threes are in their forties, fifties, or even sixties before they crash and awaken to the new story. They have a heart attack or stroke from a lifetime of overwork and sleep deprivation. Their spouses refuse to play the game of keeping up appearances while starving for intimacy and full emotional engagement. Their business nosedives in a recession or changing economic market due to events beyond their control.

Lisa Whelchel has had many epiphanies on her journey to greater self-awareness, but one especially pivotal moment came in her fifties when a relationship went wrong. She had been divorced and experienced that pain, and now another relationship had ended. This thrust her into "the terrifying abyss of emptiness" of being a Three who had conflated her identity with something and been unsuccessful at it. "When that didn't work out, I felt all the stuff that I had been trying not to feel," she said. "That I can't do anything well enough to maintain love." She worried that she'd have nothing to offer if she weren't achieving something spectacular. Without her accomplishments, she might be viewed as ordinary, boring, or unattractive. What helped her, in the end, was acknowledging the shadow of the Three, "not just the shiny parts."

Experiencing these kinds of crises and losses, Threes may feel untethered, adrift from the carefully curated life they've worked so hard to build. Perhaps up until they're faced with undeniable pain and anguish, they have not had to be in touch with their emotions or very self-reflective. They'd believed there was no reason for them to go down to the basement if everything upstairs was in working order. Suddenly, some traumatic event or unexpected loss shakes their house to the foundation and Threes don't know who they are or what to do.

If they're fortunate enough to wake up and want to change their old story before such a storm hits, then it's often the more gradual, cumulative toll of performing that galvanizes them to change. They're exhausted. These Threes are waking up troubled at two in the morning, unable to shut off their minds but also unsure of what's tripping their alarms.

Jeff Goins realized he had to change after recognizing the message of a recurring dream, one he had on and off throughout his adult life. "I'm back at college," he described, "and it's the last semester of senior year, and I'm like two weeks away from graduation. I'm looking at my transcript and I realize there's a class that I signed up for that I've never gone to." In the dream, he has completely forgotten about this science class that he hated the first day and stopped attending. There's some kind of big project due, and no way can he finish before graduation. "I think that that's how I feel when I've got a big project ahead of me," he said. "That I'm not going to finish, or I missed something and now it's going to come around and bite me, and everybody's going to see it."

Jeff tended to have this dream during intense seasons when he had overcommitted. Since he was used to pushing his emotions aside, his anxiety, fear, and stress would manifest in his dreams. Together with other moments of awareness, Jeff felt the need to make changes in his story. He had achieved success beyond what he had planned or even imagined when suddenly he knew he wanted more from his life. He wanted to know who he was apart from his achievements. He wanted to fully engage with his family. He wanted friends he could trust and with whom he could let down his guard.

Jeff is changing his old story by creating space for his new one.

Rewrite: Craft Your New Story

I'm convinced it's especially difficult for Threes to change their old story in the cultural mind-set of the US, where everything conspires to keep them swimming laps in the Olympic pool of public approval. Threes have to do the inner work to realize it's worth the struggle to float into the peace of open water under calm conditions. For this is where they will discover their true self. The solitude to cultivate their souls. The yearning for deeper connections to those they love. The power of expressing their emotions in constructive, creative ways.

What's standing in the way of such transformation is deceit, which is the Passion of the Three. Deceit doesn't mean that Threes are out in the world telling falsehoods all the time, though they may embellish their accomplishments (or, as Lisa put it, "amplify" themselves for an audience). Rather, as Enneagram teachers Riso and Hudson explain it, a Three's brand of deceit is "the tendency to present themselves in a way that does not reflect their authentic self."[4] Threes pour so much energy into fashioning an image for other people that they buy into the lie themselves, believing that the image is their true self.

The path to change and a better story for a Three, then, is the Virtue of authenticity. This is easier said than done for people who've spent a lifetime crafting a persona that was so convincing they mistook it for their personhood. Authenticity arises when Threes connect with their heart center. Threes aren't certain about their feelings and are, in fact, afraid of them; they've had a lot of years of unconsciously focusing on doing more so they wouldn't have to explore those very feelings. So, getting to authenticity involves a deep dive into their own feelings, and that means pausing to regularly take their own temperature.

While it's important for every type, committing to some kind of spiritual practice such as reflection and meditation is essential for Threes desiring change. Conditioned to remain glued to activity and productivity, *agere contra* for Threes means slowing down. They benefit greatly from habits such as meditation that require getting in touch with an inner world, with feelings, with observations and impressions missed by a story with no room for sheer joy and pleasurable entertainment. Meditation teaches us how to just be present in the world. Not to do anything but just to be.

The prospect of stopping their activity and exploring their inner life is going to sound like a waste of time to most Threes. Why do all this self-reflection when they could be getting stuff done? (In fact, Lisa shared a funny example of this: as part of her progress toward self-acceptance, she went on a thirty-day silent retreat. Perfect! But she also "found a way to jump out of it," writing 92,000 words of a manuscript so she'd have something to show for her month-long sabbatical. Yikes!)

One way they can begin to rewrite their story is to think through the inevitable consequences of *not* changing. For example, some Threes can't imagine ever retiring from work because they have no concept of life without the constant ego strokes that work provides—the next goal to achieve, project to ace, or raise to take to the bank. These Threes have neglected their inner lives for so long that they fear they'll be nothing without their careers. They have accepted the false story that they're only as worthy as their last success. As Gail Saltz points out in *Becoming Real*, that's a depressingly conditional life, one that "precludes your ever feeling adequate or enough when you aren't performing or excelling or extolling your own virtues."[5] Threes who want to change their story might ask themselves *now* whether they want to spend their golden years feeling something less than human because they are no longer working (or worse, are ill and vulnerable). Having a fulfilling life *then* depends on changing the story *now* to a more truthful reckoning of their inherent worth outside their achievements.

It also depends on allowing themselves to feel genuine emotions, including the dark, scary ones they shunt to the side while they are busy chasing accolades. "I didn't grieve until 2018," said the hip hop artist Lecrae on *Typology*. By that time, the performer was in his late thirties and had scaled the heights of achievement, breaking sales records and becoming the first person ever to win the Grammy Award for gospel music with a hip-hop album. But behind the scenes Lecrae was struggling, dealing with long-suppressed emotions about the trauma he had experienced as a child.

"I finally felt permission to be angry and upset and sad about some of the things that had happened to me," including an absent father and a history of substance abuse. He said he cried more in that one year than he had in his whole life. He stopped drinking and taking Xanax, so he had no buffer between himself and dealing with tough emotions.

"I was like, 'Whoa, I don't like this. I don't like this at all.'" But he realized that dealing with grief was inescapable if he genuinely wanted to change; there was no shortcut. "As much as I hated the grief, hated going through all of that, there's no way I'd be who I am right now" without it, he told me.

But he didn't do it alone. He knew he was dealing with acute depression and anxiety and that he needed some professional help. Like many other Threes, he found relief in working with a therapist who helped him see his inherent worth. It didn't come easily though: in his first couple of tries, he found himself trying to perform for the therapists, fashioning his message and wondering what they would think of him if he told them the *real* truth about his life. This is typical of Threes. It's especially tempting and easy for them to slip back into packaging and marketing themselves for mass consumption, even in therapy. They need someone who can see through the headlines and pop-up ads, who recognizes when they're beginning to fall back into their old, false personas and can call them out on it.

Finally, he clicked with the right therapist, who was compassionate but also not willing to settle for anything less than authenticity. She told him that just listening to all that had happened to him was painful for her. "That was what I needed to hear before I could continue," he said. Her compassion gave him the go-ahead to divulge his full history. "If you thought *that* was something, let me tell you what's really going on!" From there, the therapy took off.

Ideas for the Three's New Story

If you are a Three wanting to create a new story, think about ways to challenge your definition of true success. Setting aside the external, trophy-collecting definition of your old story, you can craft a new kind of success based on your own feelings, identity, desires, and values—not the ones you absorbed from your family and cultural conditioning.

For you, this is going to involve journaling, and some of it may be painful. Make a list of the costs of maintaining your old scripts. Which relationships are suffering because of your commitment to working, doing, and achieving? Is it taking a toll on your health? Your partner? How can you focus on connecting with the important people in your life by letting them see a little of who you really are?

As you write, reflect on what your identity is if all your awards, achievements, status props, and role descriptors are stripped away. Choose some kind of reminder—a note, an image, a sacred object—that you see on a daily basis to remind you of your true self.

As you confront your own tendency toward workaholism, make and keep boundaries between home and your job. Take breaks throughout the day—to eat, to hydrate, to meditate and catch your breath. Check in with yourself throughout the day and ask, "How do I feel right now?" Leave as close to quitting time as possible. Don't respond to work emails after you get home. Separate who you are from what you do.

Also, get out your phone or calendar and choose a date to go on vacation in the next six months, knowing this far in advance that you will not be taking any work with you. Plan to unplug and stay offline for not only minutes at a time but hours if not days (okay, you may have to work up to it). You are learning to befriend yourself, staying present in the moment without accomplishing anything. Wasting time and loving every minute of it.

You may always be inclined to win the admiration and approval of the world, but you will never enjoy contentment and soul satisfaction until you commit to nurturing your true self.

8

The Four's Story

Balance for the Romantic

"The most terrible poverty is loneliness,
and the feeling of being unloved."
—Mother Teresa

In my weekly *Typology* podcast, as I speak with individuals, couples, or panels about what it's like to walk in the shoes of their Enneagram type, I never know what's going to happen. Most guests satisfy my nearly insatiable appetite for understanding what makes people tick, but periodically, guests will surprise me with the tenderness of their self-disclosure, and the conversation becomes unusually personal and intimate.

That's what happened when I interviewed musician Ryan Stevenson.[1] He's won a Dove Award, scored three number-one singles, been nominated for both a Grammy and a Billboard Music Award, and performed to sold-out arenas all over the world. As a 6' 4" redhead, he's a commanding presence. He's a husband and father of two boys. If you met him, you would assume he felt as confident and whole on the inside as he appears on the outside.

You would be wrong.

"If I'm honest, I feel like I'm so unsuccessful," he admitted. Compared to other musicians in his genre, he felt he hadn't accomplished enough, couldn't measure up. As he approached his fortieth birthday, he was having chest pains and feeling anxious all the time.

"I have spent a lot of time wanting to succeed, and being ambitious, and wanting to prove worth, and to just show people that I'm worthy of their admiration," he explained. But, while he was grateful for the success he'd enjoyed, he was still feeling broken and inadequate. In every new situation, he would feel self-condemnation, with his initial response being "I don't belong here." Ryan felt unloved and alone.

Ryan wasn't certain about his Enneagram type: probably either the Performer (Three) or the Romantic (Four). To help us nail down his type, I asked him to tell me about his childhood.

Ryan cleared his throat. "I grew up in a tiny little farming community in Southern Oregon, out in the valley, where there was a huge divide between the 'haves' and 'have nots.' You were either a successful rancher, a wealthy landowner, or a low-wage laborer who worked for one of them. Unfortunately, my family was definitely one of the 'have nots.' My dad barely eked out a living working on a large dairy farm. We lived in a 940 sq. ft. single-wide mobile home, which was what my parents could afford at the time."

This was painful because his closest friends were rich kids and he was very self-conscious about his family not having any money.

"I was always caught in this place of definitely feeling less. I felt like I could just never really live up to their Air Jordans, and their Nikes, and their name-brand stuff. I was the generic, Goodwill, hand-me-down kid."

To make matters worse, Ryan didn't grow or hit puberty until he was almost nineteen. He stayed in the body of a fifth- or sixth-grade boy all the way to his senior year of high school. He may stand well over six feet now, but as a teenager he was bullied and mocked for being small.

"I internalized all that shame, and feeling inadequate, like the outcast," he said. "That kid has been with me until this moment. It's sad, but the voice of that little kid is still in my head, driving me to prove all those people wrong, and make them all pay for how they hurt me."

As Ryan spoke, I kept thinking about the author William Faulkner's famous observation, "The past is never dead. It's not even past."

"Ryan, if I asked you to write a memoir that captured the essence of who you are, what would you title it?" I asked. After some thought, we came up with one together: *Hand-Me-Down Boy*.

I sat up and leaned into my mic. "Now think about your life. Is the story of the hand-me-down boy who's deficient, who needs to catch up with everybody's success, true? Is the story you've been telling yourself and others about who you are *true*?"

"I don't know," Ryan said.

"That's a great answer," I responded, before gently prodding him further. "Is the story of *Hand-Me-Down Boy* still an accurate description of your life today?"

"It's part of who I am and it helped me to survive," Ryan said, pushing back.

"But you have a lot of shame and self-condemnation about things that have happened, your perception of who you are," I pointed out. "How has that helped you to survive? It sounds like it's killing you."

Ryan paused. "It's a double-edged sword. It kills me and it drives me forward at the same time," he said.

"Ryan, does God want you to live in a story that's driving and killing you?" I said, tenderly. "Does he merely want you to survive or live life to the fullest?"

"I know he wants me to live life to the fullest but something is standing in the way and I don't know how to get past it," Ryan replied.

It might sound like we all could have benefited from a drip bag of Prozac to get through the hour-long episode, but there were plenty of jokes and laughs peppered into our conversation as well. It was heartfelt from beginning to end.

By the end of the episode, Ryan and I had agreed that he was probably an Enneagram Four with a heavy Three wing—no surprise there. Like many Fours, he felt himself somehow deficient, as if he alone lacked the ability to belong in the world. As a Four myself, I recognized the contours of his old story. The good news for Ryan is that the key to transformation is adopting a better story. *Hand-Me-Down Boy* was only a first draft.

See: The Four's Origin Story

The story that Fours tell themselves in childhood reminds me of *Pinocchio*. You'll recall how the woodcarver Geppetto longs for a son and crafts a wooden surrogate, whom he names "Pine Eyes," or

Pinocchio. Shortly after his creation, Pinocchio begins to feel that something is missing and asks the Blue Fairy, "Am I a real boy?"

"No," she replies. "Not yet. You have to prove yourself worthy."

This conversation launches Pinocchio on a quest to repair his fatal flaw, to find the missing piece in his essential makeup, but he quickly gets into trouble. Though the story ends beautifully, I'll bet you that Pinocchio was a Four.

You see, Fours grow up looking for the same love, security, and affirmation every child inherently seeks. But, of course, because their parents were just as flawed and human as any others, baby Fours didn't receive what they needed and began collecting data to create their own unique personal narrative. They felt like lost children, unseen and misunderstood, cut from a different cloth entirely than the fabric of their families. Early on, little Fours didn't feel like they fit in and therefore wondered why they were so out of place. How could they be so different in so many ways than their parents and siblings? Some even fantasized that they were orphans, with biological parents similar to them who were forced to give them up for adoption.

Constantly aware of their "other" status, young Fours use their powerful imaginations and convey their oversized feelings by creating poems, images, drawings, songs, or other forms of expression. But the longing for the idealized, loving parents they never had lingers, and so, as adults, Fours are looking for ideal others who can become mentors, friends, and soul mates for them. They will often idealize people with whom they find a connection and will hotly pursue them until the other person hurts them, disappoints them, or doesn't live up to their high expectations. Once their hopes are dashed by others' fallible feet of clay, Fours quickly drop them and continue their search for the ideal other.

This pursuit to find lost love stems from a vague feeling that the Fours were abandoned at some time in early childhood, and it was their fault. Fours take a wait-and-see, hide-and-seek approach to others, particularly new acquaintances. Their relationships with others are stormy and sometimes unstable, with the Four sending mixed messages ("I love you! Go away."). One minute they're transparent, vulnerable, and seeking very deep emotional connection and the next they're withdrawn and aloof. Ironically, of course (because Fours love irony), this push-pull *modus operandi* doesn't succeed in establishing the kind of secure, committed relationships Fours yearn for. People grow tired of Fours' patterns that soon become predictable and tedious.

As Fours grow into adolescence, they often bounce from clique to clique and regularly switch interests, trying out different personae in search of a clearer sense of identity as well as the love and sense of belonging they seek from others. Used to feeling unseen and misunderstood by the world, Fours project an image of specialness and uniqueness to be seen and accepted. Some Fours have an unstable sense of identity and may have different groups of friends for each identity. In high school, I had friends in many social groups—drama club, intellectual elitists, artists, singer/songwriters, poets and literary lovers, history and government geeks, all of them. I was well liked (though I couldn't believe it) but unknown. I had grown to accept feeling different and not belonging anywhere, and I embraced the self-fulfilling isolation that accompanies such a false belief.

I told myself the story that I was the odd man out, only realizing how similar my pain was to everyone else's when I met my littermates in my fellowship of recovering addicts.

Though I didn't know it at the time, my life was governed by a long list of erroneous taken-for-granted beliefs. I remained stuck in my old story until I recognized and consciously rejected them. Here are a few of the mistaken convictions that repeatedly tripped me up:

- It's probably my fault when a relationship goes south.
- I feel things more deeply than other people.
- Life will always be vaguely disappointing.
- I'm magically special.
- Because I'm defective I'll be abandoned.
- I will be denied the love I seek.
- I need someone to complete me.
- I will never be understood.
- I don't have the magic key to happiness that other people are born with.
- I can't be ordinary.

These are broken beliefs. Nowhere in God's story does it say, "You're a misfit. You're missing something everyone else has. You're defective and unworthy of love. You'll always be abandoned. You will always be misunderstood."

This old story has to go. It's our birthright to inhabit a better narrative.

Own: The Strength and Shadow of the Four

As a Four with superpowers of imagination, musical talent, literary ability, and a wry, cynical sense of humor, I had memorized my false story before I ever composed my first song or wrote my first book.

Misfits can always find other misfits. Feeling their own personal crushing pains with the weight of the world pushing its foot on top, some Fours discover that the fastest way to alter their moods and lighten that weight is with substance abuse. (If you don't believe me, look at the list of Fours whose lives ended tragically: Kurt Cobain, Janis Joplin, Sylvia Plath, Amy Winehouse, Jackson Pollock, Judy Garland. There is no shortage of Fours who have self-imploded.)

The Four's weaknesses are not hard to spot. They're moody, and don't presume you know what they're feeling or what they're going to do next. They often paralyze themselves from acting by feeling every emotion at full volume. They desperately want to be understood, but when they *are* understood they worry that they're just like everyone else instead of unique and special.

The Four's sense of specialness can also become a two-sided weapon that they use to cut themselves both ways. On one hand, Fours justify breaking the rules, being the exception, and going against the grain because they're so unique and special. On the other, they think they deserve so much more because no one recognizes how special they are or sees how much talent, potential, intelligence, and creativity they have. Their unrecognized genius becomes proof that no one will ever understand them.

Fours are full of creative ideas, but following through can be a problem. This inability to finish can be especially irksome because Fours have so many creative ideas and inspired beginnings to novels, musicals, sculptures, paintings, projects, inventions, and innovations. Yet another irony is that Fours are especially depressed and irritable when they're not creating, but if they never finish anything they start, they only perpetuate their frustration and mood swings.

Fours' ability to feel so deeply, to register the emotions of others, and to grasp the depths of others' pain can be a huge asset in redeeming the suffering of humankind and transforming it into art. But this spongelike emotional ability comes at an enormous cost. Like supernatural empaths, Fours feel the vibe of every crowd, every meeting, every conversation, even among strangers—and this is usually overwhelming unless they learn to filter and protect themselves.

When singer and songwriter Tori Kelly came on *Typology*, she described feeling pressured to empathize even *more* with other people.[2] "If a friend was hurting and going through a really hard time, I would feel guilty for not having the right thing to say," she explained. "I would be really hard on myself and be like, 'I'm only good for writing songs. I never know what to say. I just put it all in my music.' When it comes to talk and interacting, I'm the worst." Through the Enneagram, she came to discover that "sometimes people just want you to be in their pain with them and just not have a fix for everything" and that she could do. Her simple presence could be enough. That's heady knowledge for a type who feels there is something deficient or missing in their essential makeup.

When Fours are disappointed, which is fairly often because they're prone to seeing what things ideally could be or should be, they can spiral into dark moods and melancholy. Their feelings create blinders preventing them from seeing beyond that moment and above their immobilizing pain. The world careens off its axis and they don't know how they can go on. What started as a small misunderstanding with a friend devolves into a story of wholesale abandonment.

And, sometimes, it's not small annoyances but full-on existential angst that can drive them to the edge. Fours don't shy away from the big questions about God, the meaning of life, or what happens after we die. They are unflinching in their honest engagement with the heavy stuff. One Four I know, Russell Moore (best known as an ex-leader in the Southern Baptist denomination), was suicidal when he was just fifteen years old because of his deep concerns with the authenticity of the Christian gospel.[3] "I grew up in church and belonged in the church, loved the church. I loved everything about it. But I was in this Bible Belt context where I was seeing a lot of racism and a lot of violence coming particularly from Christians, under a Christian name." It felt as if the message of Jesus had been taken hostage or was just being used as a prop for a cultural or political agenda.

It drove him to despair. "If this is all just means to an end, then that means that Jesus isn't alive. And if Jesus isn't really there, then everything that I think that I've experienced is false, which means the universe is a really dark, socially Darwinian sort of place," he thought. His faith—and, he says, his life—were saved by the writings of C. S. Lewis. "There was something about the way he was writing that I could tell he wasn't trying to sell me anything, and that there was something authentic there." It was a pivotal moment in Russell's life and faith.

Russell's comment about authenticity brings up something else about Fours: they can sniff out anything fake with the tenacity of a bloodhound. They crave genuine interactions and know instantly when other people are merely putting on a show or furthering their own agenda. They often find the authenticity they seek in music, art, and poetry. Russell's wife jokes that anyone who wants to understand him needs to listen to the music of Jimmy Buffett. Not the fun, Caribbean, wasting-away-in-Margaritaville Jimmy Buffett; more like the guy who wrote "words to make you cry" in "Death of an Unpopular Poet."

Awaken: Counting the Cost

Fours fear that it's too late to change, whether they're nine or eighty-nine. Changing their story means recognizing that they still have choices that can redirect their old story. They realize that being authentic occurs when they stop trying to prove how different they are, no matter how long they may have refused to see the truth.

The good news is that it's never too late. And it's entirely worth it. It requires waking up to all the old-story scripts that have ruled your thinking. I'm talking about lines like:

- My feelings are overwhelming because life is hard.
- The past is always with me, and I can never change.
- Everyone else manages to get through life without the existential angst that I feel.
- No one understands me or how much I suffer.
- Unless I'm special, I'm invisible.

In contrast to these statements, Fours living in a new story use their sensitivity to reach out to others and serve them with their strengths. They reinvent themselves as circumstances ebb and flow, rolling with the punches instead of absorbing them. These Fours experience a security and stability that once eluded them, remaining open-handed and keeping perspective. They accept that loss is part of life and that it happens to us all. They don't take the bruises of life personally and instead look for glimmers of hope and strands of beauty in everything and everyone they encounter.

New-story Fours can revel in the power of their emotions without drowning in them. They act more than they imagine acting. They let go of being an outsider when opportunities arise to belong and connect. They practice disciplines and habits that give their life structures and containers for the emotions, ideas, and inspirations that flood through them daily. Fours reflect the beauty of the Divine and know that no one should settle for less than knowing the same is true for them.

Unskillful Fours have an odd relationship with the past: on the one hand, they tend to wallow in it, repeatedly picking at the scabs of regrets. They think back and ruminate about their lives and what they perceive as missed opportunities—the big acting break that never happened, the soul mate that got away. Their past is jam-packed with sadness and feelings of abandonment. On the other hand, they have a strange sense that everything good that was ever going to happen in the universe already happened, and it's all in the past. As my wife says, "Ian, you're the only person I know who can see the tunnel at the end of the light!" Wallowing in regret and melancholy nostalgia, Fours don't see the glass as half-empty or half-full. Instead, we think back on the time when the glasses were made in the old country and blown by hand.

New-story Fours make an effort to live in the here and now. Instead of longing for an ideal romantic partner, they see what's good in the relationship they're in. Rather than imagining that their one true calling in life was to be a professional musician and they missed that opportunity, they keep practicing their instruments and writing their songs even if it's not going to be a career. The ability to stay mindfully present is a marker of a mature Four in a new story.

Rewrite: Craft Your New Story

Fours who are writing a new story have to confront their green-eyed monster, the Passion of their type: envy. This is not quite the same thing as jealousy. As I've tried to explain it, envy has more to do with the desire for *characteristics* that other people have, and jealousy has more to do with *things*. Fours believe that they alone lack characteristics that everyone else seems to have, some elusive key to the secret of happiness.

Tsh Oxenreider, an author and a podcaster, told me that it was when she learned how central envy is to the Four's mode of being that she was able to confirm that she was a Four herself.[4] She had just assumed everyone felt that way, that envy was a way of life for everyone.

It isn't. Although everyone has moments of envy no matter what their Enneagram type, it's Fours who have perfected envy as an art form, a way of life. Tsh has discovered an excellent hack to help her counter the envy that can rise up: she has a rule "to create before I consume." In the morning before she even glances at social media (an envy factory if there ever was one), she needs to create something, and "just be healthier by being myself." Later in the day, after she has had that time to create, she's in a better space mentally to look at other people's Instagram feeds, which are prettified to make it seem like they inhabit a perfect world.

Fours who are rewriting their story can find strength by going to the high side of One, which is the type they move to in health and security. To me, embracing the best parts of type One means that, rather than devolving into a place of reverie and twisted nostalgia where I get nothing done because my emotions are sucking up every ounce of bandwidth, I tell myself to come back to the present. To get something done, and actually finish it.

Grammy Award–winning songwriter Ashley Cleveland, also a Four, told me she resonates with that thinking about staying in the present.[5] When she goes to a dark place—which happens sometimes, as an addict in recovery—she's comforted by the fact that Four and One share a line on the Enneagram, and she can tap into the One's desire for order. "It's funny," she says. "I do not want to be an ordinary person, but I have no problem doing ordinary things. I love order and I like just having a structured day." She wakes up early, takes time to meditate, and often goes for a run. She volunteers in the community and gets out in nature. Those things "in and of themselves are just mundane," she acknowledges, "but they get you down the road." Anything she can do to step out of her own emotions and stop comparing herself to other people is a win.

Fours envy other people's contentment and the apparent ease with which they seem to move in the world. They tend to presume that other people just haven't suffered as much as they have. Other people seem to have an easier time of it. And that can sometimes give Fours a little feeling of superiority because, if they're not careful, they can become addicted to their own suffering. What becomes the core of their identity is a tragic story of the past that they don't know how to divorce themselves from—and, even if they could, who would they be without that tragic story? They'd be *ordinary*, which of course points to the underlying motivation of the Four, which is a compulsive need to be seen.[6]

Fours in a new story understand the truth about themselves: they are already enough. There's no missing link, no absent piece of the jigsaw puzzle. They belong fully in the world and can be at home in it.

Ideas for the Four's New Story

One Easter Sunday morning while I was celebrating the Eucharist at an Episcopal parish in Nashville, I looked out at the congregation and noticed a father and his ten-year-old son sitting on the aisle in the fourth pew. They were dressed in matching light-blue-and-white-striped seersucker blazers with crisp, pale yellow Oxford button-down shirts perfectly accented by satin polka-dot bow ties of navy blue.

Now, you might see this and think, "Oh, look at that father and son dressed in matching suits for Easter—how charming! They must be such an amazing, close family. I bet they're all going to Grandma's afterward for brunch and an Easter egg hunt in her backyard."

Not me. When I saw it, a tidal wave of grief washed over me. In an instant, I went from riding the pleasant tide of celebrating the holiest of rituals on a beautiful spring day to choking on my envy. There was my alcoholic father who never took me anywhere, let alone to church on Easter Sunday in matching suits, because he was passed out at home. There was my beleaguered yet steely mother who could never have gotten us all dressed and out the door in time for church on Easter Sunday.

The worst thing was, I hated myself for feeling this way. The lost boy inside me was tempted to bolt out the door in search of the nearest liquor store. I made a mental note to call my twelve-step program sponsor immediately following the service. Maybe during the postlude.

But I also heard another voice. *You know, Ian, this is just an old story, and you don't have to live in that story anymore. Be happy that little boy has a loving father. Don't go back and compare your childhood to his. You have the power and the freedom to live in a new narrative.*

My old story of envy and not-enoughness was not one I wanted to inhabit anymore.

I had come so far, with hard work and God's help and the love of so many people.

I breathed a prayer of blessing on the father-son duo: *May you have love and joy today.* I returned to the present moment, one in which I had a new and ever-present Father and hundreds of sisters and brothers who would soon make their way up the center aisle to partake in a glorious Easter meal. This is my new and better story. It tells me the truth about who I am, who we all are, deeper than our family histories and experiences.

When Fours develop and live from their true self, they're as beautiful, powerful, loving, and compassionate as any other healthy type. They realize their pain is the common denominator of humanity; no one feels entirely at home in the world. This realization contributes to equanimity, the Virtue of the Four. There's something calming about realizing they're not being singled out for suffering and therefore don't need to envy anyone else's situation. Equanimity evens out Fours' experience of pain, allowing them to experience life's ups and downs without overly identifying with any one fleeting emotional state. The word itself reflects this balance; it comes from combining the Latin roots for "equal" and "soul." Equanimity reflects a composed, emotionally balanced soul. Fours in equanimity understand they are as good as everyone else—there's no fundamental missing part—and that they no longer need to envy what other people appear to have.

To combat envy and arrive at equanimity, one of the most crucial spiritual exercises for Fours is to express gratitude every day. Practice listing blessings and gratitudes, especially each morning and evening. *Agere contra* for Fours means no longer ruminating about what's missing, what you can never have, or what you wish you'd grabbed when you had the chance. Instead, focus squarely on what you're thankful for. Start with a panoramic lens and work down to a tight close-up: being alive, a home, food to eat, coffee to drink, your pet, people who love you, work that needs doing today, transportation when needed, creative projects to actualize.

Realize that being self-critical and judgmental is often envy in disguise. Instead of focusing on what others have that you don't or finding fault in their situations to make you feel better about your own, accept what they have as theirs. If possible, celebrate with others when they achieve a goal, purchase something you admire, or enjoy a reward for their efforts. This is another aspect of *agere contra* for Fours: practice the art of sympathetic joy. That means being happy when other people are happy because you're sincerely glad for their good fortune. In Buddhism, it's one of the four highest qualities of the heart. Think of it as the anti-*schadenfreude*.

Do the creative things that feed your soul. Notice when you're bored, edgy, frustrated, melancholy, or disappointed—all signs you need to be creating something. If your day job harnesses your creativity to make a living (such as writing, designing, or performing), then find another way to express your creativity with something playful, fun, silly, trivial, or irrelevant to other areas of your life. Or, if you're frustrated because you can't make a living with your art, then find a way to express your frustration creatively.

Discover the forms of beauty that best nourish and replenish your soul: being outside in nature, listening to certain musical genres and artists, cooking a new dish from scratch, browsing in your favorite museum's online portal, planning your next trip or adventure away from home, reading certain writers (again), or whatever you know it to be. Keep in mind that there is plenty of beauty in the ordinary and mundane.

My friend Andrew Peterson, a singer and songwriter (I realize there are a lot of musicians in this chapter, but hey, I live in Nashville), has discovered a new way to be grounded—literally.[7] When he moved to a new house on several acres of land, he started paying attention to creation in a new way, wanting to know the names of the trees outside his door or the birds that would come to the feeder. When he was in the middle of a season of depression, something many Fours experience, he started building a stone wall on the property and planting new things in the soil. It was a healing experience to see new life come from what had appeared to be wintry desolation and to garnish his morning oatmeal with blueberries pulled off his own bushes. If you're a Four who wants to live in a new story, practice paying attention to the seasons and the natural rhythms of the earth. Allow them to ground you in a reality outside your internal mood storms.

Finally, be mindful of triggers that transport you to past struggles and old wounds—sounds, smells, images, places, people. Practice hitting pause as soon as you recognize the trigger and decide if you really want to think about that time your parents did whatever, you broke up with a lover in college, or you discovered that you didn't get the job.

You have a choice. Take your natural inventiveness and apply it to the creative work of a lifetime: writing your new story.

9

The Five's Story

Expansion for the Investigator

*"If you have knowledge, let others
light their candles in it."*
—Margaret Fuller

Kenny Benge speaks with fondness, and maybe even a little awe, of a gift his parents gave him when he was a child: a complete set of *The World Book Encyclopedia*. As a kid he would wake up in the morning and, before he ate breakfast or got ready for school, simply pick out a letter of the alphabet and read from that volume of the encyclopedia. For fun.

"It's hard to describe why that was engaging, but it was kind of an aesthetic experience," Kenny says. As a kid from small-town Oklahoma, he wanted to know everything he possibly could about the world. Learning gave him joy, a profound sense of connection.

His parents continued to support his budding intellect. One of their next gifts to him was a chemistry set when he was in middle school, which provided further adventures in learning about the world.[1] After he'd exhausted playing with the chemistry set, he went to the library and checked out books on more advanced chemistry experiments. Fortunately, his dad worked for a petroleum company and could bring home discarded laboratory apparatuses for Kenny to try in his makeshift chemistry lab in the garage. Kenny spent hours there, happily geeking out as he unlocked the secrets of science (thankfully, without blowing up the garage). By the time he got to high school, he knew more than the chemistry teacher.

In case you weren't convinced from this description that Kenny is a Five on the Enneagram—the Investigator, also called the Observer—he also collected road maps, picking them up from gas stations to further his quest to discover more about the world. Most Fives can relate to Kenny's early excitement about intellectual pursuits and how he sought mastery in an impressive range of fields. "Summers, I would check out eight to ten books every two weeks, read them, and then my mom would take me back." He read not just science but also sports stories, fantasy fiction—anything he could get his hands on.[2]

Socially, Kenny was not quite as awkward as many young Fives since he was good at sports and could blend in without much trouble. But he tended to compartmentalize his friends: there were the ones he knew from sports or the fellow nerds who collected rocks. He keeps his friendships separate to this day.

"I have friends that share different parts of what I like, and it seems unfair to them to impose more of myself on them than they can appreciate," he explains.

What I find interesting about this statement is that it assumes that other people might become depleted if Kenny shared his whole self with them rather than parsing himself out in doses as he tends to do. That is classic Five thinking. Since Fives are themselves drained by prolonged social interaction, particularly the kind that doesn't arise out of a mutually shared interest, they often assume that other people approach social relationships in the very same way.

Kenny, a pastor, is a very healthy Five who makes it a priority to compensate for his natural tendency toward detachment, isolation, and analysis by investing in core relationships. He is utterly devoted to his family and a few well-chosen close friends. Knowledge still thrills him, but he doesn't use it as a way to protect himself against the world.

Unlike Kenny, unskilled Fives who are living in an old story are more like someone having an out-of-body experience or the absentminded professor. They pay close attention, but from the sidelines, absorbing information that may come in handy later. Knowledge and information of almost any kind provide Fives with a line of defense against their fear. They believe the world is overwhelming and depleting and seek to impose order by retreating into their heads and relying on information to give them what most of us get from relationships—namely love, support, and community.

Whenever I've interviewed Fives for *Typology*, I remind my producer that we'll probably need to do some heavy editing—not because Fives aren't focused or compelling in their responses. In fact, just the opposite. Fives know so much and have so many ideas and thoughts at once that they begin downloading from the massive Five-Cloud in their heads, and it can take a while to go in and work their way through files and subsystems. You just have to be patient and not rush them. When they're in retrieval mode and you pressure them for a response, they will look at you with a clear-eyed poker face and say, "How can I answer you unless I have time to think?" And they're not only filtering through vast archives of neurological data but they're also organizing and arranging it to provide the best, most thoughtful, most concise response. They want their answers to be indisputable.

Fives are often not out to impress other people as much as they are committed to not looking foolish, unprepared, or unintelligent. Part of their fear-response to the world at large stems from lacking information and experience. For the story Fives form, knowledge is power, literally, the ammunition needed to battle disorder and disruption. Which explains why Fives are committed to the belief early in life that they would never have enough of what they need to survive—not only enough information but enough resources, time, money, privacy, and self-sufficiency.

See: The Five's Origin Story

The story that Fives begin to tell themselves is often in reaction to what they perceive as an intrusive, demanding world. Young Fives are typically sensitive, quiet, and introverted so when they're forced to contend with the unpredictable—like being psychologically engulfed by a parent (or abandoned by them) or the confusing social interactions of the playground, they retreat into isolation, one of the defense mechanisms of Fives. Fives have the highest, thickest personal boundaries of any type and tend to detach from their hearts and bodies into their heads.

What makes Fives become Fives is the story they tell themselves about the world being an overwhelming place they don't have the resources to handle for long stretches of time. Their reaction to what they perceive as chaotic circumstances is that they pull away from other people. It's a response to the trauma of abandonment, engulfment, or its opposite, neglect.

As children, many little Fives seem mature beyond their years, quiet, imaginative, and self-contained. Fives feel in danger of being overpowered if not consumed by other people and therefore create boundaries of their own, effectively detaching from their fearful emotions and creating a safe mental space in which to retreat. From a young age, they don't like being overly dependent on others, so they're always eager to learn new information, minimize their emotional and material needs, and practice skills that ensure self-sufficiency. They want to find answers for themselves and begin building a foundation of knowledge.

Despite their curiosity, self-initiative, and independence, Fives aren't necessarily great students in school. While their studious habits serve them well as far as performance, school creates a whole new world of uncertainty and uncomfortable situations. Peer interactions are often awkward and strained, so many young Fives end up being loners, which, of course, only reinforces their status outside the social cliques forming around them. Fives are often confused by the subjective, emotional interactions of their classmates and the power struggle to be cool and well-liked.

By the time they reach middle school, they may even study and analyze relational styles and social levels in hopes of breaking the code. When my friend Lori Chaffer was on *Typology* as part of a panel on Fives, I remember being floored by how she handled her entry into adolescence: "In junior high, I remember thinking there's a system to how people become accepted and popular, and I'm going to figure out that system." She observed the way people wore certain clothes but didn't wear them too many times in a row. So, she kept a calendar to record what she was wearing—and this is classic, it was *color coded*. "I thought, if I did this for maybe a month or two, then I would be accepted and normal." It didn't take long for her to realize it wasn't working.[3]

Such failed attempts often reinforce the story young Fives tell themselves: *The world of relationships is draining. To survive the unknown and unknowable rules of social order, I must detach and keep my head down.* Some Fives are social with people who share common interests. They might have one or two friends, often misfits like themselves, who geek out over the same things—reading all the Harry Potter books, playing marathon chess or video games, rehearsing cosplay for the new Comic-Con. These are the kids we see in *Stranger Things*, socially uncertain children whose knowledge and fearlessness save the world. Okay, so those may be stereotypical nerd exaggerations on the extreme end of the scale, but many Fives tell me they relate.

Fives grow up isolated by their circumstances or family of origin. As adults, however, some continue isolating themselves long after they have the power to choose a new story of connecting with others. But their self-reliance and competency usually carry them far into adulthood before they begin hitting the walls of their own self-confinement.

As with all types, Fives subscribe to a story that looks nothing like the Story of God, and their mistaken beliefs only reinforce their old narrative. These false beliefs include:

- It's safer to observe than to participate.
- If I open up to relationships, people will demand more than I have or want to give.
- If I'm spontaneous or express my feelings in the moment, others will disapprove and I'll feel embarrassed and out of control.
- The more I know, the safer I'll be.
- Self-sufficiency is the key to my happiness.
- Other people's needs and emotional dramas will overwhelm me.

In the passage from old story to new story, Fives have a decision to make. Do they surrender power to their old beliefs, or do they face and reject them? More important, do they see how their old story is in direct opposition to the story of God? Like the Psalmist, they need to ask themselves, "Where does my help come from?" Can they really find safety in withdrawing from the world and relying on archaic childhood strategies? Does our sacred text tell us the world is a place of scarcity rather than a place of abundance? I think not. Like all of us, Fives need to "get their story straight."

Own: The Strength and Shadow of the Five

Fives, Sixes, and Sevens make up the head triad. They share the common pursuit of finding a place of safe refuge in the world. The types in this triad create stories in response to the anxiety they experience in an uncontrollable universe. While Sixes globalize their anxiety and Sevens try to ignore it, Fives manage it through aggregating and analyzing information.

Of all the nine Enneagram types, Fives are the most emotionally detached. It's not that they don't feel things as consistently and acutely as any other type; it's that Fives seek to maintain control by acknowledging an emotion and letting it go. They may not fully process their emotions for days after an event.

Kenny described his frustration with feeling things after the fact: "I'm always jealous of people who can be immediately aware of their feelings. Once our family had a dog who was hit by a car and he died. I did a little funeral ceremony in the backyard, and my wife and kids were all weeping. So, I was kind of doing my part, you know, to be there for them. Then a while later, I was having a devotional and felt stuck until I realized how sad I felt and just started crying. But it was *two weeks* later."[4]

Kenny displayed the kind of cool, collected presence necessary in the moment, but at the expense of his own grief. This transaction is typical of Fives. They often exercise their analytical minds and clear-headedness by leading endeavors that require a steady hand at the wheel or a dogged perseverance to innovate new solutions. Conditioned by the story they've created, Fives reflexively remain calm in a crisis, which makes them good trauma surgeons, EMTs, and first responders. They're also unparalleled observers who can record what they see in artistic expressions such as photography, graphic design, and painting, often reflecting the chaotic, asymmetrical world as they see it or imposing the order they believe it needs.

Fives know how to survive and even thrive because they bring order to disorder and impose structure to what they perceive as the chaos caused by others. They use their curiosity, research propensity, and knowledge reserve to navigate into uncharted waters, willing to take calculated risks based on the over-due diligence compiled. Aware of their emotions after the fact, they tend to consider their calmness in the center of the storm around them as a strength. While others get tangled in emotional reactions, Fives calculate thoughtful responses. They're often the ones that more dynamic leaders turn to in a crisis, counting on the Five's objectivity, clarity, and larger-scale perspective.

But this has a shadow side as well because life requires improvisation.

When the story that Fives tell themselves begins to unravel, they work overtime to sustain their worldview and the necessary steps to survive in it. Adulthood usually brings more challenges and adds new layers of responsibility, requiring Fives to juggle, multitask, and often overextend their abilities. When their old story strategies no longer work, when others require authentic emotion in the moment, Fives retreat in the manner of a box turtle, clamping their shells tightly closed to keep the predators away.

Overwhelmed by life's relentless demands, Fives grow frustrated when their head knowledge is not sufficient. Whatever confidence they've accumulated may dwindle, reinforcing their perception that they must collect more data, analyze more patterns, and acquire more knowledge. They feel unprepared and become fearful, annoyed by the way others seem to crack the code of success with confident ease. Their resentment reinforces their old-story impulse to withdraw and separate themselves from that which does not compute. When their old structural systems no longer work, they don't consider it a signal to change themselves and their narrative, only their mental filters. Like buying new storage boxes or renting storage space when stuff overflows your garage, Fives, like all types, miss the obvious: *What if I no longer need all of this?*

Instead of engaging with others and fully participating, Fives often observe life from the periphery. They may be having a conversation at work and simultaneously analyzing the other person's thoughts and worldview. Or they may entertain their ravenous mental preoccupation by applying other system frames—cultural, philosophical, psychological, aesthetic, literary, and so on—to make sense of the world and impress others.

This attempt to secure a sense of mastery and exercise their mental superpowers may take on a life of its own, what Riso and Hudson call the Five's "Inner Tinker Toy."[5] Basically, they work on expanding their story into something large enough to encompass all the disparate experiences, ideas, thoughts, knowledge, and analysis they've hoarded and continue to collect. On the extreme, it can become a conspiracy rivaling *The DaVinci Code*, but usually it's more likely to be a self-consoling way to feel above the seemingly arbitrary ways of the world.

It's not surprising, then, that others may find Fives eccentric or a little odd. Again, Fives simply use these labels to shore up their belief in their own inadequacy and separateness, which amounts to justification for further self-isolation. The more others comment on their peculiarities and idiosyncrasies, the quicker Fives try to disengage and become invisible. Rather than viewing this as a defensive posture, other people may assume that Fives are simply indifferent or arrogant.

Many Fives look rumpled, disheveled, or out of sorts, as if little thought had been given to their appearance. Part of this may be their frustration with cracking the fashion trends and style codes of their peers, similar to Lori Chaffer's experience in middle school. Overall, though, Fives view clothes as functional and practical more than as expressive or stylistic statements. When my friend Dr. Andrew Root, an author and associate professor at Luther

Seminary in St. Paul, Minnesota, described his world as a Five, he confessed that the way he usually dresses is "not going to win fashion [awards]."[6] He acknowledged loving freebies, such as the swag you get at conferences and sporting events, along with hand-me-downs and gifts from others.

Lack of interest in their clothing and appearance makes sense when you consider the way Fives struggle to fit in their physical bodies. It may or may not be discernible to those around them at first, but usually others can eventually tell that Fives have a standard uniform they stick with wearing. Married Fives may love it when their spouses pick out their outfits each day, and Garanimals, the matchy-match clothes for kids from decades ago, were made for little Fives as well as Five parents. This tendency reflects their detachment from their bodies or vague awareness of being uncomfortable in their own skin, like someone wearing unfamiliar, ill-fitting garments borrowed from someone else.

In the short story "A Painful Case" from the collection *Dubliners*, James Joyce describes Mr. Duffy as a man who "lived at a little distance from his body, regarding his own acts with doubtful side-glances."[7] It's not unreasonable to suspect this character is a Five at heart, who also talks to himself about himself in third person. It's as if Fives feel contained within a vessel that they're not quite sure how to operate, resulting in a tentativeness, an awkward demeanor, and a sense of not being at home in their own bodies.

Fives often alleviate this discomfort, along with their disdain for the unexpected and unpredictable, by sticking to routines and habitual patterns of behavior. While these structural systems served them well while growing up and needing to control chaos or avoid engulfment by others, by adulthood they can become rigid, obsessive, and dysfunctional. Fives don't want friends dropping by unannounced—not because they're naturally inhospitable but because their normal routines are disrupted. They don't welcome houseguests easily and may feel drained by the anticipation more than the actuality of visitors.

Andy Root explained, "It's really hard for me to have anyone even stay at our house. I just have the hardest time." If his wife, who's a helpful, gracious Two, wants to ask her sister and her sister's kids to stay over, "I need three weeks to a month to get my mind around what that would possibly look like and how that could happen. It just feels invasive, to be quite honest." The way he deals with anxiety and the demands of work is to become very private. "I need my house and I need this little room to go to," he said. "I'm okay with my immediate family, but the thought of even having a good friend over for dinner just feels like an incredible burden."

What Fives often fail to realize, though, is that their old story burdens them even more.

Awaken: Counting the Cost

If Fives don't hit pause on their old story, the cost manifests primarily in their relationships. Others don't understand them—something Fives tell me they hear a lot—and story-tranced Fives don't believe they should have to justify themselves to anyone. Their lack of emotion in the present moment leaves those around them wondering why they're so unfeeling or detached. When Fives attempt to express appropriate social reactions based on the cues of others, they may come across as aloof or intellectually superior.

Being detached from the immediacy of their feelings typically takes a toll on those close to Fives. My buddy Joel Miller told me a perfect example: His wife Megan, who's a Four, "will react in a moment very viscerally to something and I won't. She'll look at me then and say something like, 'I'm so tired of getting angry *for* you.'" Megan struggles to understand how Joel is immune to the impact of something that affects her so powerfully. His feelings are there, but they're like pieces of a puzzle he's trying to sort and fit together.[8]

When the partners and friends of Fives are not as patient as Joel's wife, then they may eventually give Fives an ultimatum or simply abandon them and move on. Fives then use such losses as reinforcement for their same old story about how scary, harsh, and unpredictable the world is. If even those closest to them can't be counted on, then who can?

In their careers, Fives may become experts in their field—they store so much knowledge, how could they not?—but if they are not evolved Fives, they struggle to apply it effectively or to take necessary risks to collaborate with other team members. They become loners whom others perceive as antagonistic, difficult, or stubborn. These Fives may have more expertise and inside knowledge than anyone else in their company, but they're reluctant to share it. Desiring to stay securely in their comfortable, cruise-control lane, they can be passed over for promotions if they are seen as colleagues who are excellent sources of information but not leaders.

The more Fives cling to their secure-only-because-it's-familiar narrative, the more they isolate themselves and become even more disconnected. Anything that disrupts their expectations and routines—basically anything requiring them to get out of their head—becomes a threat. Their story becomes an obsessive burden, and their mental landscape, which they consider the only safe place, disintegrates into darker fantasies and idiosyncratic fixations, something out of a Stephen King novel, which is only fitting from a fearsome Five himself. In fact, King has often commented that he writes his stuff to get it out of his head. Instead of retreating alone into his worst fears, he found a way to externalize them and share them with millions of readers. It's a great example of what happens when Fives stop believing their old story and create a new one.

Rewrite: Craft Your New Story

Committing to a new narrative requires Fives to face their fears and get out of their heads. They slowly realize that, as adults, they can erect more permeable boundaries against engulfment and fearful chaos and respond in ways unavailable to them as children. That doesn't mean they will entirely stop retreating from the world when it becomes overwhelming, but it means they can be intentional about balancing the demands of relationships with their own need for solitude. Musician Dan Haseltine of the band Jars of Clay, a Five, says that when they were on tour amid the constant grind of travel and performing, he had his ways of staying sane.[9] "I would go and get in the bunk and put on headphones and listen to music. I spent a lot more time in the dressing room." And, sometimes, he would engage in managerial tasks, just to stay busy—and by himself. "That was the way that I kept myself at a distance from the people around me and the fans and everything," he said.

Fives in a new story discover that their understanding, insight, and curiosity can be harnessed in service to people and causes outside themselves. Open-minded and less fearful, they slowly dip their toes into the pool of the deep emotional waters within, gradually immersing themselves and discovering that they will not drown. Instead, they discover the joy of floating on the surface as well as swimming through choppy currents. The subterranean cave of emotions buried deep within becomes more manageable—still scary at times but worth the effort to integrate.

I see this kind of integration in Tim Mackie. He's a self-identified theology nerd: a seminary professor and one of the two founders of the Bible Project, a creative approach to making the Bible understandable to ordinary people via short, smart, funny animated videos. And, throughout his life, he has dealt with the typical Five issue of detachment, seasoned with regular dollops of anxiety from his Six wing. His academic training, he says, "just cemented me in my neuroses and more unhealthy habits" as a Five.[10]

But at age thirty-six, Tim became a father, which introduced "this really important season of self-discovery. It's forced me to find new tools to help me understand why I behave the way I do towards these little humans I live with."

Becoming a parent has made him more open to receiving emotions as they come—even viewing them as a gift. When I interviewed him, he related a recent experience of watching the Pixar movie *Inside Out*, which is all about emotions, with his family. One of the plotlines deals with a forgotten toy from the main character's childhood, which exists only in the deepest recesses of the character's memory. Sitting there with his sons, then ages four and six, Tim suddenly felt overwhelmed by how much of their childhoods they would not remember, how much would be lost forever.

Tim began to weep uncontrollably.

"It was like my body was just overtaken by grief and loss. My wife was just staring at me. I never cry. And she was like, 'What on earth is happening to you? Are you okay?'"

He was more than okay. He was captivated by the beauty of the movie and was "letting these losses and the victories of their lives form and shape more emotional awareness." And he was experiencing those emotions in the present moment, not saving them up to analyze later. This is a step toward living in the new story for Fives.

Ideas for the Five's New Story

Tim's cultivation of experiencing the depth of his feelings in the now rather than hoarding them for later brings us to the Passion of the Five: avarice. Now, avarice for a Five is not about material gain or fancy living. Fives are hardly the poster children of conspicuous consumption. Rather, it's about conserving emotional resources that the Five feels are precious. Most Fives feel they only have so much energy to go around—and it's not as much as people of other types. So, they titrate it drip by drip, allocating only a bit here and a bit there. They are overly protective of their time. They also hoard knowledge and feel that, if they can just acquire enough of it, they'll be safe.

Fives in a new story should ask themselves, "When is enough enough?" They learn to set limits when surfing online or completing projects. As hard as it might be to finish, they stop researching and storing information and simply start applying and doing. Instead of going into their heads when afraid, bored, or insecure, developed Fives find ways to take action.

To counter avarice, Fives in a new story cultivate their type's Virtue, which is nonattachment. Nonattachment may seem an ironic Virtue for this type that seems pretty nonattached already. How much more withdrawn could they get? But remember that Fives' aloofness is rooted in the fact that they *are* attached to their own need to be self-sufficient and in control of their environment. The Virtue of nonattachment isn't about disconnecting further from people but realizing why they desired to cut themselves off in the first place. Real nonattachment, according to Enneagram teacher Helen Palmer, "requires that you have a full range of feelings available to you."[11] Fives in a new story are seeking that full range of feelings.

For example, healthy Fives find a way to connect their overdeveloped minds with their underdeveloped body awareness. Many of them find meditation, breathwork, yoga, and tai chi helpful practices that help them bridge the gulf created by their old-story, out-of-body habits. Others explore hobbies and sports that require them to engage mind and body in harmony—painting, sewing, woodworking, swimming, dancing, biking. As they become more present in each moment, they grow in confidence and security, delighting in the beauty and wonder of the smallest details around them.

Fives who are growing toward their Virtue of nonattachment experiment with giving of themselves more extravagantly than they're used to. Reach out to people who are important to you for no reason other than to let them know you care about them and value their relationship. Call or text a friend and agree to meet for drinks after work or dinner together this week. Make it clear you have no agenda for your time together except to spend time together. Trust me, they'll be delighted that you took the initiative. Also, be deliberate about venturing out of your comfort zone by giving a talk on a topic you haven't fully mastered yet, volunteering to lead a committee, or auditioning for a role in a local production. Let others experience your true self and all you have to share with them.

Work on experiencing your emotions as they arise. Throughout your day, pay attention to what you feel in any given moment rather than sending all emotional data to your internal processing unit for later analysis. Practice expressing your emotions spontaneously and, when appropriate, sharing them with others.

Trust that you have an abundance of yourself to give. You are more than enough.

10

The Six's Story

Courage for the Loyalist

> *"I learned that courage was not the absence*
> *of fear, but the triumph over it. The brave*
> *man is not he who does not feel afraid,*
> *but he who conquers that fear."*
> —Nelson Mandela

When disaster strikes, you want a Six nearby.

They are prepared and then some, having already imagined all that could go wrong and thinking through escape routes, survival plans, hiding places, fire escapes, underground bunkers, and tornado shelters long before they're needed. They know the Heimlich maneuver and how to tie a tourniquet. Sixes are often lifesavers, literally, and feel validated when they get to apply one of the plans they've formulated in order to survive.

I can't tell you how many Sixes I've heard recount the most amazing stories in which they handled some crisis because they were mentally, if not physically, prepared for such an occasion. I remember leading an Enneagram workshop in New York City once when we were discussing this very superpower of Sixes. A woman raised her hand and said, "Okay, you're not going to believe this, but on the way over here, I was walking down the street and imagining what I would do if a terrorist in a van drove up on the sidewalk. Where would I run? Would I go into a store? Would I run into the street to get out of the way?"

She also wondered how many people would be hurt in this hypothetical terrorist attack and how she could best help them. Where would she be most useful to the most people? Would anyone need CPR? (Good thing she took that class.)

While this slide into immediate concern may seem dramatic—especially since she was problem-solving about a situation that hadn't actually occurred!—it's typical of many Sixes, who often advocate for those in need. They are called Loyalists because of their deep desire to uphold justice, fairness, equality, and traditional values. They want to know what's expected of them and what their role will be should a crisis occur.

Jill Phillips, a singer-songwriter from Nashville who is a Six, told me, "I sort of assume that people are thinking about my common good in the same way that I'm thinking about theirs.[1] I'm super loyal. I would say I have long friendships with people. . . . We get involved in our communities and our neighborhoods and that sort of thing." And for Jill and other Sixes, the phrase "our communities and our neighborhoods" refers to the entire *human* community, not just people from two blocks over.

Like Jill and my Enneagram workshop participant, at their best, Sixes are reliable, dependable, valiant upholders of what is right and good. They're troopers and guardians, questioners and truth-seekers, devil's advocates and doubting Thomases. They know what to do in a crisis and have more plans for surviving disasters than any doomsday prepper living off the grid.

In their worst-case stories, however, unskilled Sixes make fear their idol, with power to control them both actively and reactively. They believe corruption and conspiracy threaten to destroy us all at any minute. With fight or flight as their only options, these Sixes inevitably are controlled by their fear and insecurity.

See: The Six's Origin Story

Every child may struggle with the fear of being abandoned by mom and dad and unable to survive on their own. For Sixes-in-the-making, however, this unconscious fear becomes the central theme of the story they create to survive such a possibility. They unconsciously come to accept the idea that they can't possibly make it on their own as irrefutable fact, not personal opinion. They need the parental authority's umbrella to feel safe and secure, and if it's not there (or not perceived to be there), then Sixes experience raw panic. Instead of retreating into their minds like neighboring Fives or buoying past their fear like optimistic Sevens, young Sixes take the head-on approach: they assume they can't trust their own judgment, leaving them in a chronic state of anxiety.

To alleviate the stress caused by this belief, Sixes often look elsewhere and pledge loyalty to whomever and whatever they think can protect them and provide security. They're loyal for a reason, at least initially, receiving whatever strength they're convinced they're unable to provide for themselves. Like all types creating a false belief and clinging to it as a narrative guide, Sixes practice the same self-perpetuating, circular reasoning. They believe they don't possess the inner compass to make decisions without the support of others, so they turn elsewhere; this process of turning elsewhere for advice further confirms their doubts about their own judgment.

Growing up, impressionable Sixes become magnets for anxiety. They're quick to heed warnings from overly protective adults and assume there's a basis in reality for every sensational danger they see online—flesh-eating plants, murder hornets, and still-water rip-tides, not to mention drive-by shootings, rabid dogs, and gas leaks in homes just like theirs. One Six I know read an article years ago about people who were trapped on the subway for hours in a dark tunnel, so she started carrying a tiny flashlight in her purse for just such an occasion. (PSA for all non-Sixes: It's not enough to have a phone flashlight. Flashlight apps drain a smart phone's battery life alarmingly fast, so you need a backup plan. Sixes are the kings and queens of backup plans.)

John Mulaney, a stand-up comic and former writer for *SNL*, does a hilarious set about the annual assemblies at his school while growing up.[2] The problem was the recurring guest speaker, a detective with the Chicago police department, there to discuss safety precautions and public vigilance. As Mulaney points out, though, it's hard for eight- and nine-year-olds to process the news that would-be kidnappers roam the streets. Of course, these *are* real dangers and kids must be taught to be wary of strangers and to look for red flags signaling imminent danger. For Sixes, however—and I'm guessing Mulaney would include himself—such messages only pour fuel on the fire of their already fearful imaginations.

It's not only from well-intended adults that little Sixes form their stories. Many times, they absorb the tense atmosphere at home from a parent whose behavior may have been unpredictable, sending a volatile message to children craving security and stability. As a result, these kids learn the warning signs and keep careful watch on erratic behaviors and threatening situations.

Many young Sixes won't express their fears and worries overtly and instead simply prepare carefully for what they think might happen. They're keen observers who will pick up on the vibe of others, often relying on how others regard a situation to determine its potential for danger. They watch a few kids jump off the diving board before deciding whether to get in line. They're willing to take risks or face their fears as long as their peers precede them.

Insecure about their ability to face life's fears alone, Sixes create a story in which they need to follow standards established by credible authorities. They value and trust the people entrusted to care for them who do their job well. Careful listeners, they like following leaders who respect them and explain the rules and, more importantly, the reason for the rules.

Formative Sixes may gravitate to safety in numbers by joining sports teams or close peer groups that appear to offer security and order. Lacking confidence in their own inner compass, however, they don't often take risks, which is a shame since occasional leaping before looking could potentially provide the self-assurance they so desperately need.

Once they realize that not all adults and authorities can be trusted, however, young Sixes become conflicted. As much as they may want to believe in the power of others charged with serving and protecting them, there will always be uncertainty. Because some people cannot be trusted, all people have the potential to betray or abandon the Sixes in their care.

This awareness that ultimately no one can be fully trusted at first may exacerbate the way Sixes approach life's dangers. While many remain apprehensive about life's many triggers for harm, others react and tilt toward the opposite extreme, dismissing potential fears or actively demonstrating mastery over them. The first group are often called *phobic* Sixes and the latter, *counterphobic*. The situations avoided by phobic Sixes may be pursued with daredevil passion by their counterphobic peers. They still believe their story about the world being so dangerous that every day could be like an episode of *24*. But counterphobic Sixes train to be Jack Bauer and meet that challenge, eager to go against conventional authorities who represent potential threats.

Sixes are on a continuum between phobic and counterphobic. They form a story at a young age that combines the two and sends them ping-ponging back and forth depending on the situation. In the morning, they may be heralding their boss and believing everything is great at work and that same afternoon they may fall into anxiety that their job is going to be displaced by robots. At the heart of their narrative, Sixes commit to becoming fear's dance partner, sometimes following and sometimes taking the lead.

Sixes constantly question themselves and others. It would help them if they questioned the old ideas and faulty beliefs that keep them stuck in their old story. To inhabit a larger, more beautiful story, Sixes need to cross-examine and debunk their old ideas, like:

- I'll be safe if I prepare for the worst.
- If I worry and plan enough, everything will turn out okay.
- It's hard to not doubt or to trust people when so many of them have hidden agendas.

- I can't trust myself to make good decisions.
- I'll always be filled with doubt and worry.
- I won't be safe or certain unless I have something or someone outside myself to trust and be loyal to.

The story Sixes tell themselves isn't the story God tells. If left hidden and unchallenged their faulty beliefs will eternalize their old story. The phrase "do not be afraid" appears 365 times in scripture. Sixes who want to live in a better, truer story have to surface and put the screws to their unconscious assumptions: "Does God want me to believe that I'm alone and defenseless in a chaotic and uncertain world? Does God tell me to be anxious about everything? Does God want me to believe it's up to me to protect myself?" Sixes who want to make the passage from their old story to their new one need to practice answering these questions (and others like them) with a full-throated, "Hell, no!" (It's okay, God won't mind.)

Own: The Strength and Shadow of the Six

One of my favorite Sixes is Sarah Thebarge, a Yale-trained medical professional, international speaker, author, and humanitarian. When I brought up phobic patterns, she confirmed the tendency of Sixes to anticipate and prepare for disaster. "I can't go anywhere without knowing where the emergency exits are," she said.[3] "When I'm on an airplane, like when I was flying back and forth to college from the East Coast to LA where I was going to school, I would not drink anything that had ice in it, and I would not eat anything on the six-hour flight, because I just did the math. If you choke, if your airway gets occluded . . . they can't land the plane in time."

She'd arrive in LA "really hungry and thirsty, but at least I wasn't going to choke to death!"

Sarah also pointed out another benefit of the chronic anxiety suffered by most Sixes. "One of the best things I've read about Sixes is that because we have so much fear and anxiety about little things all the time, that when it comes to big things, Sixes are often the most brave and the most willing to jump in. We spend all day every day overcoming fear. When it comes time to put that muscle into action and do something good, we're ready."

Depending on how developed they are in handling their response to fear, Sixes can make great leaders, crisis negotiators, and first responders. While other types may feel blindsided by an unexpected turn of events, most Sixes assume something will go wrong and plan accordingly. Good thing, then, that more people are Sixes than any other type on the Enneagram, perhaps reflecting the universality of fears for all human beings.

Obviously, when they stick to their old story, Sixes can become paralyzed by the intricate alarm systems they must maintain. When they stick to their old script, they struggle to see beyond living in fear because of life's inherent dangers—which are relentless and always present, now more than ever. I've frequently mentioned that our world today seems more dangerous and volatile, partly a result of the immediacy of social media, online connectivity, and the subsequent ceaseless news cycle. These factors only intensify the volume of ambient anxiety Sixes hear on a daily basis.

While I was writing this book, several events caused us all to feel like Sixes, primarily the COVID-19 pandemic and the potential collateral damage of quarantines, dwindling resources, and economic recession. For months, people sheltered in place, hoarded toilet paper, watched the death count spike dramatically, and panicked whenever they felt the slightest tickle in their throat. News coverage became a political minefield compounded by the lack of scientific understanding of the novel coronavirus. That same year, our country faced another kind of pandemic as systemic racism collided with police brutality. Protests went on for weeks punctuated by occasional riots, looting, counter-protests, and political grandstanding. Then there was a highly polarizing election, with a president of the United States making baseless claims of voter fraud and inciting a violent takeover of the Capitol building in Washington, DC.

In other words, who the hell wouldn't be scared?

For the Sixes I know, however, the pandemic and civil unrest stripped away any veneer of control and stability in society. Some of them told me that, for the first time in their lives, the actuality of their experience was worse than anything they had imagined. Many suffered from heightened anxiety and sank to the bottom of the depression barrel sooner than the rest of us. While almost everyone suffered anxiety and depression, Sixes often felt hopeless and helpless. If they had endured some kind of childhood trauma, the pandemic became a significant trigger.

On the other extreme, if not sidelined by unprecedented fear, Sixes poured themselves into busyness like never before, refusing to acknowledge the sheer terror lurking in their imaginations with a kind of counterphobic bravado. Many of these were the neighbors you saw building new decks, delivering food to the elderly and those at high risk, or sewing masks for their loved ones. No matter how hard they worked, though, they never felt it was enough to adequately prepare.

Stubbornly clinging to their old story, Sixes felt no choice but to succumb to fear.

Awaken: Counting the Cost

When Sixes refuse to create a new story, they pay a steep price. Dealing with chronic anxiety often results in exhaustion on every level. Physical health suffers because the body does indeed keep the score, as a classic contemporary book on trauma reminds us.[4] Stress, fatigue, and compromised immune systems set the stage for a host of diseases and dysfunctions. Sadly enough, diagnosing the results only intensifies the cause, producing more anxiety and distress.

Intimate relationships can be difficult for old-story-suffering Sixes. As loyalists, they long to commit to someone they can trust and depend on. Alongside this desire, however, they unconsciously doubt that their partner is as committed to the relationship as they are. Their insecurities cause them to wonder why their partners would want to be with them or invest in a long-term relationship. They get caught in what my *Typology* guest Francie Likis describes as the internal conflict of being a Six: "It's hard for me to make an important decision, but I don't want you to make that decision for me. Right? I'm scared you're going to leave me, but I don't want to be dependent on you. So, it feels sometimes like a lot of push and pull."[5]

Sixes who are ready to live in a new story start by waking up to the reality that most of their fears don't actually material-ize. Are you listening, Sixes? The vast majority of the things you spend time ruminating about in your brain never come to pass.

Singer-songwriter Jill Phillips summed this up perfectly when she returned to *Typology* for a solo interview.[6] "Any terrible thing that's happened to me, I didn't see coming," she said, while the terrible things she catastrophized about possibly happening didn't. What she has learned from that over the course of many years is to have faith.

"Something happened and I didn't see it coming, and yet God was faithful, and I got through despite my weakness and my fear. The accumulation of those experiences has made me a very different person."

Most Sixes eventually recognize that they must develop wellness plans and coping strategies if they're ever going to enjoy their lives. They realize the impact their mixed messages have on others and work to resist them as well as to communicate what they're feeling when triggered. Once they commit to doing the work and discarding the story that once felt like their only lifeline, Sixes often bloom into life with a distinct beauty that rivals any other type.

Rewrite: Craft Your New Story

Many Sixes acknowledge that facing their fears in order to change their story got harder before it got better. But seeing their worst fears realized can sometimes have a liberating effect. That was the case with another guest on my all-Sixes panel, Leslie Jordan.[7] She shared how it took a Job-like year of loss and lament to bring her to a point of clarity and change.

"The year 2016 for me was the realization of a lifetime of fear," she said. The year began with a miscarriage at six weeks, and it ended with a surgery to ascertain whether she had thyroid cancer.

In between she weathered the chaos of some leadership changes at work and family drama at home. "Everything in my life felt turbulent and unsafe. There were days where I literally was laying on my back on the floor." In those times, she felt like she simply could not get up, and that her worst fears had come true.

Then she began to rally, thinking about how much power and authority she had long given to her worst-case scenarios. She began questioning the way she tended to look to her husband or the church or other people to give her reassurance. In hindsight, there was a gift in all the terrible things that happened that year: she realized that through it all, the faithful authority she needed was God. She also realized her own strength, that she was capable of surviving one of her own worst-case scenarios. "I didn't lose my faith and I didn't lose myself in the process," she said in wonder. The worst had happened, and she proved strong enough.

As painful for Leslie as those events were at the time, she made a choice not to let her old story keep her on the floor. She discovered a strength and resilience she didn't know she possessed until all her other resources had been stripped away. Leslie's story encapsulates a sacred journey from the Six's Passion, which is—you guessed it!—fear, to the Six's Virtue of courage. She gained the courage to face her fears herself, without relying on an external authority figure to guide her in what to do, and she learned that she could survive the worst-case scenario. She could dare to trust herself.

Courage is key for Sixes who are ready to change their old story. In fact, Sarah Thebarge shared a brilliant distinction that helped her push through her fears. As a medical professional who travels around the world, often to underdeveloped regions broken by war and poverty, in order to provide treatment, medicine, and preventive measures, Sarah not only has to endure those scary, marathon international flights but the unknown variables sure to disrupt her plans once she lands. A cancer survivor as well, Sarah clearly has had to look her demons in the eye and stare them down. She had a revelation a few years ago. "Whenever I get ready to do these international trips, or I'm going to dangerous places, people tell me, 'You're so brave!'" It bothered her, that word "brave," and she wondered how it was different than the word "courage." So being a word nerd, she looked it up. Being brave, she learned, "is when you don't feel afraid, so you take big risks and do dangerous things. Being courageous is when you feel all the fear but you choose to do it anyway because there's something more important at stake."

Amazing, right? That, right there, is the very definition of what *agere contra* looks like for Sixes: choosing the Virtue of courage when your natural makeup is wired for fear. Sarah redefined courage in a brilliant way that all Sixes would especially appreciate. "I'm not brave," she said. "But what takes me to these places is courage. It's choosing something that matters more to me than being safe and feeling secure. These people who are suffering matter more to me than my life."

This kind of courage is what makes developed Sixes so special. We see its wavering formation in iconic scenes like Thomas doubting that Christ had resurrected until he saw for himself or Hamlet wondering if he really saw his father's ghost outside Elsinore. In literature and theology, politics and social activism, music and movies, commentary and satire, Sixes reveal the fears we all have and help us get a handle on them because they know them so intimately.

Sixes who are rewriting their story can also take heart from recognizing what a gift their strengths are to the world. Their characteristic loyalty is amazing.

I once met a woman who is a Catholic nun, a social activist, and a self-identified Six. She could see how the strengths of her personality type had helped her remain a steadfast member of her religious community.

"I'm part of a church that's confused and threatened by women," she told me. "People have asked me, 'Why don't you leave? You could join the Episcopal church and enter one of their religious orders. Chances are they'd ordain you to the priesthood if you felt called to it.'" Instead, she decided, "Rather than abandon my tradition I've chosen to stick with my family of faith to help bring about change from the inside."

This woman was expressing courage by remaining where she was, even though she realized her church might never fully recognize the gifts of women in her lifetime. That is the remarkable kind of loyalty Sixes routinely devote to people and institutions.

Ideas for the Six's New Story

New-story Sixes carry themselves with a new-story confidence because they endured their dark nights of the soul frequently enough to know that light returns in the morning. They discover they no longer need anyone else to protect them or provide authority. Like Sarah and other developed Sixes, they find a cause bigger than their fears that liberates them from their old script.

If you are a Six, try limiting the sources of information you absorb on a daily basis, especially worst-case scenario stories in the news. Realize that whatever information and entertainment they provide must be worth the price of having those sounds, images, and details forever in your consciousness.

As you manage your fears, identify the difference between actual fear linked to a clear cause in the moment versus the chronic, unspecified anxiety you experience most days. Condition yourself to dial down the ambient anxiety each day and to acknowledge the actuality of legitimate fears that require decisive action. To raise your awareness of these patterns in your life, regularly (once a week, if not daily) spend some time journaling about the worries and fears that plague you most frequently. Describe your insecurities and worst-case outcomes. But make sure you conclude by listing times when you endured unexpected hardships, overcame impossible odds, and persevered to conquer your fears. Don't forget to include times your preparations prevented problems or allowed you to handle unpleasant surprises.

Think carefully about the power you cede to other people. Whom do you unquestioningly trust the most or look to for reassurance about your decisions? Which authority sources or figures do you tend to react *against* immediately, and why? Part of cultivating the Virtue of courage means learning to trust yourself, which means allowing for mistakes or missed opportunities as you grow in confidence. You may not always make perfect decisions, but let them be *your* decisions.

Finally, get involved in your community. One of your greatest gifts is the stability and loyalty you bring to the people around you. And finding good causes to uphold isn't hard for transformed Sixes. As you become stronger, more confident in yourself, and more willing to take courageous risks, you become a guardian of all in need of protection and a first responder for humanity. Katie Williams (an interior designer in Nashville who was on our podcast with a panel of women, all friends of mine) summed up the heartbeat of liberated Sixes better than anyone I know when she said that we're all called to lay down our differences. That's the essence of the Gospel for her, that we're all in this together, coming together for one another. No matter color, age, differences of any kind, whether in neighborhoods, towns, nations, the world, "seeing all of those people helping each other makes my heart soar. . . . That's what it's all about."

During these times when the unimaginable happens daily and the unexpected is the only constant, Sixes may be facing do-or-die moments more often than other types. Their old horror story no longer works because reality has superseded it. So, they have the opportunity to create a new epic, a heroic tale of overcoming adversity and triumphing over old self-imposed restrictions. Sixes can be our freedom fighters, not running from fear and not reacting against it, instead acknowledging fear with healthy respect while stepping forward to do what needs doing.

Because Sixes know what *courage*—not just bravery—is all about.

The Seven's Story

Depth for the Enthusiast

> *"Face your life, its pain, its pleasure,*
> *leave no path untaken."*
> —Neil Gaiman

He wants to go to a monastery, and I want to go to Mardi Gras."

With that one simple, yet brilliant, observation, Shauna Niequist revealed so much about being a type Seven on the Enneagram. She and her husband, Aaron, are bestselling authors, innovative thinkers, and longtime friends. They're also big fans of the Enneagram, so when they were willing to swap stories, I loved hearing more about the dynamics of their relationship, especially because Aaron is a Four, like me.[1]

Turns out, their relationship has been a unique study in contrasting styles since they first met. Shauna and Aaron worked together and actually started their first jobs out of college on the same day. They were hired by a large church and "worked this totally bonkers student-ministry schedule," Shauna said. Right away, they had a good sense of each other and how different they were. "Our team teased us that we were the most opposite people in any meeting. That in any meeting situation, if there were two options, I'd pick A and he'd pick B 100 percent of the time."

Being the Romantic, Aaron wasn't thrown off by their opposing views and admits it may have added to his attraction to Shauna, who was "this very pretty girl." He finally asked her out for a Saturday date, and she accepted. Then, on Friday at the end of the workday, he said he would pick her up in the morning. "And she's like, 'Yeah, so I also invited Brian to come with us.'" There he was thinking they could connect and have this shared experience together, and she didn't even realize it was a date and assumed the more, the merrier.

Obviously, they eventually started dating without others tagging along, but their distinct personality styles and different expectations followed them into marriage. Aaron and Shauna shared how they each reacted recently when faced with an unplanned Labor Day weekend. Coming off of a busy time of traveling, speaking, and working, Aaron needed some downtime and just wanted to relax, be alone, and write a song or create something. Shauna, on the other hand, said, "I want to go on a boat with a lot of people. I want there to be watermelon, and maybe cheese and crackers, and music. I wanted to get sandy and sunburned and have a super-fun, extended family kind of wild, busy, windblown weekend."

That would be the whole monastery and Mardi Gras thing.

Shauna's preference is straight-up Seven. Sevens are caffeinated from birth. They burst into any room with an exuberance that turns heads. Their eyes twinkle and their lips hint at the smile they're about to give you. Sevens are the pied pipers and raconteurs, the self-help gurus and sales reps who know what you need before you do and make you feel honored to buy it from them. The story they tell themselves could easily be titled *At the End of the Rainbow—There's a Pot of More Rainbows (and a Blue Unicorn)*.

No wonder then that everybody loves Sevens, myself included. While I know Sevens don't have it made and no Enneagram type is better than another, I still love the way they bring the joy juice. Surely, irreverent humor originated with a Seven as well as travelogues, adventure vacations, and the power of positive thinking.

My son, Aidan, is the quintessential Seven. He's twenty-four, but he still gallivants wild-eyed through the world, laughing like a baby who's just discovered his toes.

It wasn't until Aidan began wrestling with the inevitable, difficult realities of adulthood that I got an up-close look at the price Sevens pay for always skipping and jumping through life. His challenges gave me a higher-resolution picture of the way Sevens, like every other Enneagram type, have a flawed story that eventually falls apart. There's a price for their often unhinged positivity that can't be paid until they face their true losses.

No one can manufacture optimism continuously without sacrificing a part of their humanity. Life's challenges are unavoidable and produce seasons of loss, disappointment, and wounding. Just because they're not acknowledged and owned doesn't mean that you ducked life's punches. Sevens prefer to suffer privately rather than letting anyone else see them bleed, especially themselves. In order for healing to ever occur, there needs to be a time of feeling the pain, dressing the wounds, and allowing scars to form. Human beings need to experience the full spectrum of

their emotions without getting stuck in any one range or ignoring the other half.

See: The Seven's Origin Story

It's hard to know what a Seven's origin story actually is. They put
such a rose-colored filter on everything, including their childhood,
it's hard to separate fact from fiction without double-checking
with their other family members. Sevens aren't compulsive liars;
it's simply that they have selective memory. Many recount enjoying idyllic childhoods in safe neighborhoods with loving parents,
golden retrievers, and close pals with whom they built tree houses,
splashed in local pools, and made memories to last a lifetime, or
at least until the next school year. When pressed, Sevens may acknowledge cracks in their photoshopped histories and wear a vague
smile about family financial struggles, absent parents, sibling rivalry,
and dropping out of soccer to form a garage band that broke up a
couple months later when they joined the French Club in order to
go to Paris on spring break. Even as they correct details or sharpen
blurry memories of their upbringing, most Sevens are still embel-
lishing to delight their audience.

When told with the manic delivery of a Robin Williams,
childhood stories simply become fodder for a Seven's repertoire.
Heartbreaking facts are so coated with sunny-fied observations and
brilliant humor that any tears shed are usually from laughing, not
crying. The thing to keep in mind, though, is that originally Sevens used their smarts and rapier wit to protect themselves from the
painful truth. If they could laugh about it, entertain other family
members by spinning a tale about it, and repeat it often enough,

then whatever happened couldn't be so bad, after all. They refuse to know what they know.

Sevens unconsciously told themselves that they had to figure out a way to avoid the unpleasant emotional and psychological ache of events beyond their control. The glare from always looking on the bright side blinded them to the harsh realities they were committed to avoiding. Whenever I've been in a difficult emotional space and talked to a Seven, they always seem baffled why I would stay in my mood. After their attempts to pull me out of myself fall flat, they get frustrated and quit wanting to hang around with me. It's as if anyone else's pain reminds them that the same dark chasm waits somewhere inside them.

The severity of painful events likely varied, but young Sevens lumped them all together. If one twinge might lead to a sharper ache and then to a chronic discomfort, better to avoid that slippery slope entirely. The story that Sevens first began crafting centers on the same reaction to fear that their fellow triad members, Fives and Sixes, encountered. Like these other two types, Sevens likely wove their tale when some dynamic in their family of origin went sideways. It may have been their parents' divorce, mom or dad's addiction, a sudden and unexpected move, or the special needs of an ill sibling.

In light of not getting what they needed, Sevens took authorship of their own narratives with a fierce determination to nurture and soothe themselves. They created the first choose-your-own-ending story by committing to "happily ever after" endings and what they had to believe to get there. If their parents or other caregivers couldn't provide what they needed, then Sevens would find it in new adventures, in special interests and hobbies, in fascinating ideas and conversations, and in like-hearted friends. With their distractible minds bouncing from person to person and thing to thing, young Sevens told themselves that any deprivation could be overcome by positive distraction. No matter what kind of tragedy or drama swirled around them, they told themselves that they could make their story into a comedy, farce, epic adventure, or fairy tale. Through sheer willpower and creative force of imagination, Sevens transform *Girl, Interrupted* into *The Princess Bride*.

The old adage is true, though. If you don't live your story, then your story will live you. Sevens can only postpone the painful parts of their lives for so long before they become the source of the sad story they worked so hard to avoid.

It's a long list of mistaken beliefs that prevent Sevens from fully entering their new story:

- I can't endure feeling bored, trapped, locked into a routine, or FOMO.
- I must have multiple escape options.
- If I get trapped in feelings of pain or deprivation, I'll never find my way out.
- I can't depend on anyone for anything—especially for supporting me when I'm in pain.
- I should be exempt from having limitations and restrictions imposed on me.
- Charm is the best first line of defense.
- No one can be trusted to satisfy me. I am on my own.
- What I really want can't be found in the present moment or inside myself—it's always outside and in the future.

These bogus beliefs prevent Sevens from entering the Larger Story of God. It's hard for them to hear that we have a God who opens himself to suffering, that Jesus is the Suffering Servant, that the more we avoid pain the less we become like him. But it is a life-saving truth for Sevens that we have Someone we can depend on in our time of need, who will stand with us in seasons when we must walk bravely through pain, not around it.

Own: The Strength and Shadow of the Seven

With their insatiable appetite and zest for life, Sevens possess an arsenal of strengths for survival. They often see their role as being a catalyst, someone who injects enthusiasm into any venture. Others gravitate to them because of their gift for reframing negatives into positives. A few years ago, I visited my Enneagram Seven (with a Seven wing) friend Bob Goff at his waterfront home in San Diego. One night we stood on the dock behind his house, quietly enjoying the sunset. Eventually, Bob broke the silence with, "You know, Ian, if I ever saw a shark, I'd just tell myself it was a dolphin with teeth." See what I mean?

Entering adolescence, Sevens find themselves the center of attention among peers as well as adults, teachers, coaches, recruiters, and casting directors. They often possess the poise and star quality to become natural leaders—on sports fields, in theater spotlights, and on music performance stages. Others want to be them and be with them, knowing that Sevens will at the very least turn boredom into bedlam. Even if they've just arrived in town, Sevens always know where the parties are, or at least that they can start one anywhere, anytime. Their intelligence, wit, and curiosity have the magnetic power to pull others along for the ride without needing to have a destination.

Sevens are spontaneous, outrageous, and innovative when it comes to finding ways to be the center of attention, often making them exceptionally successful in a marketing-driven, PR-fueled, social media-accelerated world. Because they are so committed to avoiding limitations and pessimism, Sevens come up with unique points of view and overlooked solutions. They are masters at mining silver linings out of the deepest, darkest caverns of pain and disappointment, refusing to see value in the power of grief and lament.

Instead, Sevens love taking on something others find depressing, boring, or debilitating and turning it inside out until they find its opposite. They know that working this kind of magic forces people to see the subject matter differently as well as the one casting the spell. These are the stand-up comics who can turn the ingredients panel from a cereal box into a side-splitting sketch. The managers who look beneath dropping sales numbers to find the reason in order to create a new pitch or product. The language teachers who make learning effortless by comparing slang, idioms, and swear words while slyly slipping in usage, pronunciation, and grammar.

I saw this kind of creativity at work when former pastor Rob Bell started his first church at the beginning of his career. Instead of playing it safe and looking at inspiring Gospel passages from the New Testament or tried-and-true Sunday school stories from the Old, Rob launched a study of Leviticus with a small group in his living room.[2] Now, I don't know how to describe this third book of the Bible to you if you're unfamiliar with it, other than to say it's not where most readers turn for spiritual comfort. I would be doing a terrible injustice if I called Leviticus the biblical equivalent of operating instructions for your new flatscreen TV remote, but there are some parallels. Basically, it's a book of rules and rituals for maintaining religious, legal, and moral principles among the Hebrew people, newly liberated from bondage in Egypt after 400 years. To most people, it's dry and tedious, but in Rob's hands, Leviticus came alive in graphic, relevant, brilliant ways like never before. People loved it, begged him to keep going and do an entire series on it, and came in droves, quickly outgrowing his house.

A lover of the Violent Femmes, Banksy, rabbinical literature, paddle boarding, and sneaker couture, Rob's success as a pastor, author, speaker, and event creator resulted from bringing the unexpected to his pulpit. Here's the way he characterized his Enneagram type: "A Seven is the first person to believe that the action's somewhere else." In a way, that sense opened his mind and heart to spirituality. "From an early age, I had a deep sense of wonder and awe that there's more going on here. The basic sort of reductionist materialism always felt like going from color to black-and-white." And everyone knows that black-and-white is no fun. Although Rob's Seven-ness opened his eyes to the "more, more, more" sense of the wonder of the universe, it also drove him nuts that "it needed to be run through the filter" of a religious establishment. Rather than ceding spirituality to the establishment, however, he grabbed the microphone himself, creatively and tirelessly reimagining what it means to do church.[3]

Anyone who spends much time with a Seven knows that their contagious energy cannot be suppressed. They're Tigger unleashed on the rest of us Poohs and Eeyores wandering around the Hundred

Acre Wood. Whether mentally, physically, creatively, or emotionally, the other types will always struggle to keep up. When Bob
Goff and his wife, Maria, a serene and lovely Nine, sat down with
me, she said, "Living with this man is like living with a power
plant. The minute he wakes up in the morning, it's like the power
plant turns on and he's just ready to go. It doesn't matter if he's got
a cold or if he's just survived malaria, or he's got a thousand things
to do that day—he's just up for it."[4]

Maria nailed it: Sevens don't multitask—they *simulti*task, doing a
million things simultaneously, mentally if not physically, all the time.
As an attorney, philanthropist, international humanitarian, university
educator, bestselling author, world-class speaker, and walking travel-
ogue, Bob is a great example. The man always has so much going on
that I feel embarrassed to ever call my schedule busy. With so much
boundless energy, constant mental activity, and irons in every fire,
Sevens indeed seem like the type you want to be.

Until you peek behind the curtain and realize that their wizard
is just as screwed up as you are.

It takes enormous fuel to keep a Seven going, or at least that's
the story they tell themselves. Enough is never enough. They're
always seeking stimulation and on to the next new experience, the
next big thing. Boredom, stillness, and restlessness are anathema
for Sevens so they tend to overcommit and cram their schedules as
full as their minds. Each day should be filled with as many pursuits,
pleasures, and passions as possible. Each twenty-four-hour finite
unit holds the potential for infinite possibilities.

Aware of their own capacity for doing so much at once and
always future-tripping, Sevens constantly seem surprised when the
rest of us cannot keep up. When I've been at events with Sevens,

they sometimes overlook the way others live at a different vibrational frequency. Most people can't keep up with them and aren't willing to try, leaving Sevens to conclude once again that they are responsible for meeting their own needs.

Supercharged and leading the pack, they struggle to connect with others in ways the rest of us take for granted. Especially with spouses, families, and close friends, Sevens get frustrated just hanging out and doing nothing. But part of experiencing human intimacy is the ability to be silent together, to rest, to experience the present moment alongside other people. Hitting pause to enjoy those moments, however, shuts the power plant down and allows the possibility that unpleasant thoughts, feelings, and memories might slip in. Better to skate just ahead of the cracks and outrun anything that might slow them down. If that leaves others behind and results in more loneliness, then all the more reason to go faster.

Sevens chafe at being forced into routines and repetitions and will find a way to escape confining situations. They work cleverly around people or systems that they perceive will impose limitations on them or ask them to conform. They need options and possibilities, hidden passages out of the boxed-in world they sometimes encounter with others.

Even when they appear to conform, Sevens find a way to rebel. They're the people appearing to take copious notes during the mandatory work conference who are actually writing their novel. They're the entry-level employees organizing the office pool for the Super Bowl. These aren't necessarily problems until bosses or co-workers pull rank and want Sevens to fall in line. Then Sevens will find a way to maintain the integrity of the old story they tell themselves by seeking stimulation and escape elsewhere—often through substances or process addictions.

Addictive behavior, in fact, symbolizes the theme of the Seven's false narrative, an impatient demand for instant gratification in order to avoid their fear of never having enough of what they think they need. This is the perfect recipe for addiction, or, if not then for what the Enneagram has traditionally labeled the Seven's Passion: *gluttony*.

Not necessarily for food, although many are epicures and foodies, but an insatiability in all their appetites. Nothing is ever enough—food, drink, success, sex, celebrity, and status symbols. The tragic irony, of course, is that the more they throw into the empty hole inside, the deeper it grows. Frustrated that they can no longer keep their shadows suppressed, Sevens become reckless and out of control, careening between extremes of manic behavior and anxiety.

As amazing, creative, dynamic, inspiring, and innovative as Sevens can be, there is no way for them to maintain those qualities without counting the cost and confronting their shadow. Facing their defects of character is uncomfortable and frightening work for folks who want to avoid pain. "What you most want to find," it's been said, "will be found in the places where you least want to look."[5]

Awaken: Counting the Cost

If it's not a descent into addiction that sends a Seven to a breaking point, then it's because they come up against an experience they can't positively reframe. Eventually, they will hit a wall forcing them into self-awareness and self-care. It's not a matter of *if* but simply *when*. It might be triggered by an illness or injury to their overstressed but underattended body, the collapse of several projects or endeavors at once, or simply the kind of mental fatigue that comes when the circuits get fried from always running at max capacity. Relational failures and confrontations or interventions from spouses and friends sometimes force Sevens into finally doing the inner work they've been skirting their entire lives.

In addition to rest, stillness, and reflection, coming to terms with their insatiability is also paramount. Rob Bell explained, "Sevens think if we could just get over there. If we could just make this or accomplish that." Then Sevens would be happy, the theory goes. But Rob knows it's a mirage. "It's like the Jay-Z song, 'Onto the Next One'—it's living in anticipation of the next great high."

Sometimes experiencing too much too quickly can be a true silver lining for Sevens, not just their spin on a breakdown. "At some level I was blessed with . . . what's perceived as tremendous success early," explained Rob. He had "an existential crash very early on" when he started wondering, *Where does this go?* He was meeting more people and doing more travel and getting more accolades "and none of this was going away. It was just worse than ever." Over time, though, Rob recognized the key to changing his story as a successful but unhappy Seven: "I'm actually missing out on life with all of what is seen from the outside as success. I'm missing it. Missing it."

As a result of awakening to his old story, Rob, like all developing Sevens, began making new choices that forced him to reduce options and focus on what he does best and cares most about. Sevens know they're maturing when they stop to catch their breath and start saying no to themselves without regret or second-guessing. Taking time to examine their lives, they come to terms with key losses and unacknowledged trauma. They grieve what they didn't have in childhood that they should have and accept that there's nothing they can do to change the past. They realize that there is nothing out there that will fulfill them—not hanging out with the Dalai Lama, climbing Everest, starting another YouTube channel, walking the *Camino de Santiago*, or buying more designer footwear.

Unfortunately, many Sevens don't count the cost of their old story until they rip the binding. They bottom out. Their spouse or partner leaves them for someone deeper, more willing to reflect and build intimacy. Their body demands rest and attention. Once they turn the corner, though, Sevens enjoy the balance that comes from accepting all their emotions and experiences. They discover that routines and structure can stimulate growth as much as change and innovation. They realize just how much they can give others if they're willing to tap the brakes and focus.

Once they're willing to start a new story, Sevens realize the real adventure has just begun.

Rewrite: Craft Your New Story

Sir Richard Branson has been quoted as saying, "If happiness is the goal—and it should be, then adventures should be top priority." Spoken like a true Seven who has conquered business and has his eyes set on space travel. But Sevens don't need to go to the moon to create space for their new story. Once they're willing to examine their default settings, slow their pace internally as well as externally, and experience the present moment, they discover the peace that has previously eluded them. They discover that the greatest adventure truly lies within. One way to think about it is that Sevens often have FOMO, or fear of missing out on the next adventure, the next opportunity, the next experience. But new-storied Sevens realize what Rob Bell did: what we want is already here and we'll miss it if we don't look within.

There is often a deeply spiritual component to their new story, which I believe is required for all types' transformation but especially for Sevens. Sevens inhabiting the Larger Story believe that God will support them when difficult situations and feelings arise. They realize that they are not alone and that other people do, in fact, meet many of their needs. Bigger is no longer better, and innovation does not always trump tradition. Fasting from the overload of stimulation they relied on, mature Sevens relish their sense of being present without distraction. Shauna Niequist expressed it beautifully, "It's almost always healthy when I say, 'I can go without that. I choose not to do that. I choose slower, I choose quality over quantity. I choose to connect with one as opposed to many.'"

Shauna is describing a signature aspect of the Seven's Virtue, which is sobriety. Sobriety doesn't sound like much fun, conjuring images of dour or puritanical teetotalers who want to spoil a party. But sobriety is the way of freedom for Sevens. It's about resisting the constant temptation for more, more, more and resting in the knowledge that there is already enough. As Enneagram teacher and author Alice Fryling describes it, "sobriety means taking only what we need."[6] Sober people don't run away from pain but recognize it as a fact of life that only makes them appreciate joy all the more.

Since avoiding pain is a way of life for unevolved Sevens, honoring pain with a seat at the table is going to take a willful act of *agere contra*. But as Sevens discover the freedom that comes from accepting pain and suffering as part of life, they grow into vibrant individuals with even more appeal. They no longer have to be the center of attention and can listen to others and hold space with them in the midst of loss or heartache. These new-story Sevens don't have to entertain and amuse others who are struggling but can come alongside them. They take time for themselves and practice being present. Rest and Sabbath become part of their schedules to restore and maintain balance. Living out their new stories, Sevens are still agents of creation and curiosity. They continue to delight the rest of us with their spontaneous humor and brilliant insights. Their childlike wonder awakens hope in us.

Ideas for the Seven's New Story

Realized Sevens have a depth and gravitas in their new stories that help them experience the richness of life and the full spectrum of human emotions. They are no longer running—from themselves, from their pain, from the truth. They accept that there's nothing this world can offer them to fill the hunger inside their hearts. Gluttony and emptiness have been replaced by sobriety, spiritual nourishment, and service to others. They embrace the suffering of others as their own and offer newfound strength that doesn't need to say a word. At last, they can simply be.

If you are a Seven seeking that kind of peace, start with the basics. Take an honest inventory of your go-to excesses—eating, drinking, collecting, shopping, traveling, gambling, surfing Instagram, or whatever you run to rather than feel disappointment, pain, fear, and anxiety. Make a plan for practicing moderation that includes support and constructive accountability from other people.

Find a way to practice solitude by getting away from others and being alone with yourself. Use the time devoid of distractions to ground yourself in the present and consider what your life means and what you want it to mean. Try journaling at least two or three times a week and focus on the unpleasant feelings, situations, and conflicts you've been avoiding. Describe them in open, honest ways without being funny, ironic, sarcastic, entertaining, or profound. Your journal is not an audience. Don't be surprised if you find all the fears you've been suppressing rising up to the surface. Just acknowledge them and know they're normal.

If, like many Sevens, your energy sends you pinging off in multiple directions, part of cultivating sobriety is to work on mindfully being present for one thing or one person at a time. As you consider everything on your to-do list each morning, choose three as your priorities to tackle before moving on to any others. Push the rest to another day's list. At the end of the day, look over your list again and be proud of what you completed.

Practice habits that help you follow through rather than race ahead. Finish the book you're reading before you start another one. Don't buy another pair of running shoes until you've worn out the last pair you bought. Complete that short story before diving into the novel you want to write.

Also, commit to regular physical exercise to burn off energy and calm your mind. Workouts with repetitive motion—swimming, hiking, biking, surfing, paddle-boarding, rowing—are great for allowing your mind to relax and sort through your usual mental radio-dial chatter.

Know that, in your core relationships, you have much to offer others beyond being the life of the party. The next time you start to cheer up someone with your charm or humor, hit pause and take a breath. Think for a moment whether cheering up is really what they need in that moment. Consider listening, accepting, and comforting them without using anything from your usual bag of tricks.

With a willingness to reflect and redirect their focus, new-story Sevens discover the strength to confront and process their sadness and pain. They no longer avoid confrontations or resist accepting blame and owning responsibility. They display a grounded wisdom that allows them to stand secure, no longer running away from what could not be escaped. As Sevens grow and cooperate with their new narrative journey, they begin writing a tale worthy of their true self.

The Larger Story

We Live by Mending

> *"All my favorite people are broken.*
> *Believe me. My heart should know."*
> —Over the Rhine

A few years ago, my artist friend Mako Fujimura presented me with one of the most extraordinary gifts I've ever received—a broken nineteenth-century tea bowl. *What a pal*, you might think to yourself. *Did he give you dead flowers as well?*

But this was no ordinary piece of pottery.

One-hundred-fifty years ago, the despondent owner of this broken cup had taken it to a master craftsman who repaired it using the ancient method of *kintsugi*, the Japanese art of restoring damaged ceramics using tree lacquer dusted with fine golden powder.

The tea bowl took my breath away. Rather than disguise the spider web of cracks, the craftsman had filled them with glinting gold as if to highlight and celebrate them. Paradoxically, the result was a bowl transformed into something more resilient and beautiful than it was prior to breaking. According to tradition, the grateful owner would have taken the cup home and proudly displayed it in a place of honor where it could be seen and admired by visitors.

"Man is born broken. He lives by mending. The grace of God is glue." That's what the playwright Eugene O'Neill once said through a character in his play *The Great God Brown*, and he was right. Like the damaged tea bowl, all of us are broken. It's okay. It's not our fault. It's the way the world is. But there's good news—like a kintsugi master, God can mend the fissures in our hearts by filling them with restorative grace. He can make us "better than new."

The Larger Story

Not long ago, I was invited to speak at a large church conference about how modern worship leaders could incorporate ancient liturgy and sacraments into their Sunday services. I ended my talk with a celebration of the Eucharist, demonstrating how Holy Communion could be contemporized and usher people into God's presence. But to be honest, I wondered if my presentation would connect with 1,500 twenty-two-year-old worship leaders who were accustomed to performing four-song worship sets backed by killer bands, on stages with arena lighting and lyrics projected on jumbotrons.

As it turned out, though, the experience was profoundly moving for me and the skinny-jean-clad assembly I had grown to love over three days. At the end of the service, I went into the auditorium to express my gratitude and say goodbye to the conference attendees. But then I glanced up at the stage where I had presided at the Eucharist and noticed that the leftover Communion bread was no longer on the table. I was sore afraid.

In the Episcopal tradition, consecrated communion bread is considered sacred, and either has to be consumed by the priest or carefully broken up and reverently returned to the ground. When I asked the conference organizer where the bread had gone, he said, "I think the stage crew threw it out."

Jesus had left the building.

Two minutes later, I found myself at the bottom of a dumpster, sloshing around in a foot of fetid water while a group of confused, nondenominational worship pastors watched me rescue round loaves of swollen communion bread bobbing about like wine corks in a sea of garbage juice. I was a wee bit grumpy.

But then it struck me. Of course Jesus was in the trash—this is the crux of the Larger Story of God! It's the true tale of a God who willingly plunged into our fallen, often dumpster-ish world to restore and redeem us. Though we still bear life's inevitable cracks and scars, God fills them with luxuriant love, making us resplendent. Now, like the pierced risen Christ, we can proudly display our mended wounds to the people of the world and announce that they, too, can be restored.

But what's our part in the bargain? To see and deconstruct the old story we've told ourselves about ourselves, to own our beauty and brokenness, to awaken to the ways our old story has limited us, and to boldly rewrite a new narrative that aligns and fits inside the larger, redemptive Story of God.

But there's more.

As my sponsor Jack said, transformation begins when we "let God do for us what we cannot do for ourselves." Allowing grace to disburden us of our broken, archaic childhood stories looks different for every type.

When Improvers find a home in the Larger Story, they realize that God's love for them is not predicated on their accomplishments in perfecting themselves, others, and the world. That's the underlying premise of their old, soul-crushing narrative. They'll know they're living in a new story when they become more conscious of the Passion of anger that has ruled their lives and naturally begin to experience the Virtue of serenity that comes when they accept that the world is "perfectly imperfect." And so are they. They can be both riven and redeemed. Be encouraged Improvers: most of your mistakes are misdemeanors, not felonies! As Julia Child once said, "If you're alone in the kitchen and you drop the lamb, you can always just pick it up. Who's going to know?"[1]

Helpers who inhabit the Larger Story of God know that God's love and the love of others can't be won through strategic giving. That's their worn-out, self-told myth. They believe the promise that God loves (and likes) them without terms. Helpers who have found a home in God's Story have awakened from the trance of their Passion, pride, and learned to practice the Virtue of humility. They freely admit that, like everyone else, they need help to navigate life and they don't have the resources to help or rescue everyone. They remember that even Jesus took naps. They can rest.

Performers in God's Larger Story are finally convinced that their value doesn't come from endless productivity, achieving goals, or winning the admiration of the crowd. New-storied Performers are no longer haunted by the question, "What more do I have to do or accomplish before I can know I'm esteemed by God and others?"

Now they trust God's pronouncement, "I love you: I want you to be," as Saint Augustine wrote. Because they've rejected their Passion's siren call of deceit and cultivated the Virtue of authenticity, restored Performers no longer mask their true self to fool the world into believing that they're the paragon of success. They have tasted the joy of authenticity. They're home.

Romantics living in the Larger Story of God know they're seen and worthy of belonging. They have loosened their grip on feelings of deficiency or abandonment. Their quest for the unnamable "missing piece" is behind them. Now they revel in their original goodness and completeness. Romantics inhabiting God's Larger Story continually let go of the Passion of envy—comparing themselves to others and feeling inferior. Because they no longer over-identify with their oversize feelings, they can practice the Virtue of equanimity. Now they stand firmly and calmly in the gale of life's storms. They're finally willing to be happy.

In the Larger Story of God, Investigators realize that retreating into the fortress of their mind will not give them ultimate security or safeguard them against the draining demands of our intrusive world. As they move away from the Passion of avarice and embody the Virtue of nonattachment, they're no longer held hostage by the fear that they don't have sufficient energy or resources to live life fully. They are no longer attached to the beliefs, behaviors, or objects they used to believe would protect them: minimizing their needs, limiting the time they spend with people, or hoarding knowledge, privacy, material resources, personal information, and physical space. In the Larger Story of God, they've relinquished their scarcity mindset and connected to the abundance found in the interconnectedness of all things.

When Loyalists jettison their old story and subscribe to the Larger Story of God, they take to heart the words of the author Frederick Buechner, "Here is the world. Beautiful and terrible things will happen. Don't be afraid."[2] In their new story, Loyalists release their grasp on the Passion of fear and embrace the Virtue of faith. Now they're confident that God holds them in his hands *and* they're certain that they have the inner wisdom and strength to face the dangers of life as well. New-story Loyalists are more decisive, and they don't over-rely on outside people or things for guidance. They have faith in God and in themselves.

Enthusiasts who reside in the Larger Story of God no longer feel an inner emptiness that they frantically need to fill with more (and more and more) to avoid feeling pain. They're consciously aware of their Passion of gluttony and set their sights on cultivating the Virtue of sobriety. Inflamed desire for intellectual stimulation, amusing exploits, thrilling experiences, and fun has cooled. These new-story Enthusiasts are learning to live in the truth of the present moment. Exploring the full range of human feelings and experiences—both pleasant and painful—is proving to be the greatest adventure of all.

Challengers who inhabit the Larger Story of God have seen and owned how the Passion of lust has controlled them. Now instead of moving against others, they move bravely toward them with an undefended heart. No longer afraid of re-experiencing the pain of the past, new-story Challengers cast off the Passion of lust and embody the Virtue of innocence. Childlike, they open themselves to the world, experience the simple pleasure of being alive, and trade in their own willfulness to know and follow the will of the Divine.

Peacemakers who live in the Larger Story of God know they matter. Rather than merge with the agenda of another individual or the group, these Peacemakers become individuated human beings with a sharply etched clarity of their own voice, their own desires, their own preferences and priorities. These Peacemakers no longer shuffle through the world in the Passion of sloth but stride toward the Virtue of right action. Now they invest in their own self-development. Rather than recoil from conflict, they appreciate its power to make connections. They bless the world with their tranquil presence.

Abandoning our old story and entering God's Larger Story is arduous work. It takes time. You might be tempted to look back with regret on all the years you spent living your unhappy fiction and believing lies about yourself and the world that caused you and others pain. When this happens, remember the words of Maya Angelou, "Forgive yourself for not knowing what you didn't know before you learned it."[3] I often find consolation in these words.

Finally, believe not only in God, but also in yourself. You can do this. When the fear of casting off your old yet comfortable story overwhelms you, or you worry that you might fail in this holy enterprise, remind yourself, "The one I am becoming will catch me."[4]

There's a mantra-like blessing I like to whisper over all the people I see walking past me on the streets of my hometown, Nashville. I say it over fellow travelers as I wend my way through crowded airports. I intone it in coffee shops, and even extend it to people who cut me off on the highway. And now I invoke this amended blessing over all of us as we embark on our quest to inhabit the larger, better, and truer story that awaits us.

May we have love.

May we have joy.

May we have peace.

May we have healing.

May we have rest.

And may the release from our old stories into the freedom of our Larger Story be a journey filled with hope and renewed faith in the possibility of irreversible transformation.

Acknowledgments

This book could not have been written without the love, patience, support, and kindness of my long-suffering wife, Anne.

My grateful appreciation also goes to my literary agent and unfailing champion, Kathy Helmers; my brilliant editor, Jana Riess; and Dudley Delffs, whose writing help in the early stages helped get this book off the ground. I'm thankful for the work of Mickey Maudlin and the editorial team at HarperOne, and proud that they gave this book a home.

In my day-to-day work I would be lost without my assistant, Wendy Nyborg; my dear friend and *Typology* podcast producer, Anthony Skinner; my management team, Jay King, John Meneilly, and Morgan Careny; my business manager, Jason Childress; and my twelve-step sponsor, Steve L., who has saved my life more than once.

I also want to thank my kind and supportive friends, especially Steve and Deb Taylor, Randy and Katie Williams, Michael and Julianne Cusick, Chris and Laurel Scarlata, Mary Gauthier, Ashley Cleveland, Reverend Becca Stevens, Reverend Scott Owings, and my St. Augustine's Chapel family. I'm grateful to my "spiritual support" dogs, Percy and Pip. Finally, let me express my humble gratitude to all who bravely shared their stories on *Typology*.

Notes

Chapter 1: The Stories We Tell

1. From Robert Bly's translation of Johann Wolfgang von Goethe's poem "Holy Longing," in *Eight Stages of Translation: With a Selection of Poems and Translations* (Chicago: Rowan Tree, 1983).

2. Ian Morgan Cron and Suzanne Stabile, *The Road Back to You: An Enneagram Journey to Self-Discovery* (Downers Grove, IL: InterVarsity Press, 2016). To listen to my podcast, *Typology*, visit typologypodcast.com.

3. Carl Jung, *Collected Works of C. G. Jung, vol. 8: Structure and Dynamics of the Psyche* (Princeton, NJ: Princeton Univ. Press, 1976, 2014), paragraph 784.

4. Mo Willems, *Goldilocks and the Three Dinosaurs* (London: Walker Books, 2012).

Chapter 2: Changing Your Story

1. Donald Miller's interview has been edited for length and readability, as have all of the *Typology* excerpts. The original conversation can be found in Season 2, episode 14, November 1, 2018, https://www.typologypod cast.com/podcast/2018/28/06/episode2–014/donmiller; and Season 2, episode 15, November 8, 2018, https://typology.libsyn.com/part-2-don -miller-on-directing-your-new-story-enneagram-3-s02–015.

2. Donald Miller's foreword to Scott Hamilton, *Finish First: Winning Changes Everything* (Nashville, TN: Thomas Nelson, 2018), xi.

3. James Hollis, *Finding Meaning in the Second Half of Life: How to Finally, Really Grow Up* (New York: Penguin, 2005), ch 1.

4. Cynthia Bourgeault, *The Wisdom Way of Knowing*, quoted in Beatrice Chestnut, *The Complete Enneagram: 27 Paths to Greater Self-Knowledge* (Berkeley, CA: She Writes Press, 2013), 38–39.

5. "Passion," Online Etymology Dictionary, https://www.etymonline.com /word/passion. Enneagram teacher Christopher L. Huertz also makes this point in *The Sacred Enneagram: Finding Your Unique Path to Spiritual Growth* (Grand Rapids, MI: Zondervan, 2017), 76.

6. Oscar Ichazo, *Enneagram of the Passions* and *Enneagram of the Virtues*, explained in "The Traditional Enneagram," https://www.enneagraminstitute .com/the-traditional-enneagram. I've substituted "authenticity" for Threes instead of "truthfulness" as in Ichazo's version.

7. Chris Cruz interview, *Typology* Season 2, episode 16, November 15, 2018, https://www.typologypodcast.com/podcast/2018/15/11/episodes02–016 /chriscruz.

8. Julianne Cusick interview, *Typology* Season 1, episode 49, June 21, 2018, https://www.typologypodcast.com/podcast/2018/21/06/episode49 /juliannecusick.

9. I'm a big fan of Gail Saltz's book *Becoming Real* and employ some of her ideas here along with those of various wise Enneagram teachers and some of my own. See Saltz, *Becoming Real: Defeating the Stories We Tell Ourselves That Hold Us Back* (New York: Riverhead Books, 2004), especially chapter 11.

10. Edmund Lo, "*Agere Contra*: Why Go the Opposite Way?", Ibo et Non Redibo: A web-log of Canadian Jesuits, April 2, 2014, http://www.ibosj.ca /2014/04/agere-contra-why-go-opposite-way_2.html.

Chapter 3: The Eight's Story

1. I wouldn't presume to diagnose my mother retroactively, but I suspect her speech delay may have been caused by trauma.

2. See "Einstein Syndrome: Characteristics, Diagnosis, and Treatment," by Dorian Smith-Garcia, medically reviewed by Karen Gill, MD, in *Healthline*, https://www.healthline.com/health/einstein-syndrome#what-it-is.

3. The nature-nurture debate has been a long and contested one. I believe the formation of the human personality is a confluence of both.

4. Ian Morgan Cron, *Chasing Francis: A Pilgrim's Tale* (Colorado Springs, CO: NavPress, 2006), 68.

5. Cron, *Chasing Francis*, 67.

6. Sasha Shillcutt interview, *Typology* Season 4, episode 29, January 7, 2021, https://www.typologypodcast.com/podcast/2021/07/01/episode04-029 /sashashillcutt.

7. Viktor E. Frankl, *Man's Search for Meaning* (Mumbai, India: Better Yourself Books, 2003), 64.

8. Helen Palmer, *The Enneagram: Understanding Yourself and the Others in Your Life* (San Francisco: HarperOne, 1988), 316.

Chapter 4: The Nine's Story

1. Mike McHargue interview, *Typology* Season 1, episode 23, December 14, 2017, https://www.typologypodcast.com/podcast/2017/14/12/episode23 /sciencemike.

2. Chris Gonzalez interview (panel of Nines), *Typology* Season 1, episode 7, August 17, 2017, https://www.typologypodcast.com/podcast/2017 /08/17/episode7/panelof9s.

3. Audrey Assad interview, *Typology* Season 4, episode 34, February 11, 2021, https://www.typologypodcast.com/podcast/2021/11/02/episode04-034 /audreyassad.

4. William Paul Young interview, *Typology* Season 1, episodes 36 and 37, March 22 and 29, 2018, https://typology.libsyn.com/036-wm-paul -young and https://www.typologypodcast.com/podcast/2018/29/03 /episode37/paulyoung.

5. Seth Abram, telephone conversation with Jana Riess, March 8, 2021. Find Seth at *Fathoms: An Enneagram Podcast,* https://fathoms.podbean.com/.

6. Alina Bradford, "Sloths: The World's Slowest Mammals," Live Science, November 26, 2018, https://www.livescience.com/27612-sloths.html.

7. Newton's Laws of Motion, https://www1.grc.nasa.gov/beginners-guide -to-aeronautics/newtons-laws-of-motion/.

8. Anne Bogel interview, *Typology* Season 1, episode 32, February 22, 2018, https://www.typologypodcast.com/podcast/2017/22/02/episode32 /annebogel.

Chapter 5: The One's Story

1. Amy Julia Becker, *A Good and Perfect Gift: Faith, Expectations, and a Little Girl Named Penny* (Minneapolis, MN: Bethany House, 2011), 57.

2. Amy Julia Becker interview, *Typology* Season 2, episode 23, January 3, 2019, https://www.typologypodcast.com/podcast/2018/03/01/episode02

-023/ajbecker. For more information on *gastroparesis*, see https://www
.mayoclinic.org/diseases-conditions/gastroparesis/symptoms-causes/syc
-20355787.

3.   Amy Julia Becker, *A Good and Perfect Gift: Faith, Expectations, and a Little
Girl Named Penny* (Minneapolis, MN: Bethany House, 2011), 33.

4.   Lee Camp interview, *Typology* Season 1, episode 5, August 3, 2017, https://
www.typologypodcast.com/podcast/2017/08/03/episode5/leecamp.

5.   Julianne Cusick, email to author, May 20, 2021.

6.   Richard Rohr and Andreas Ebert, *The Enneagram: A Christian Perspective*
(New York: Crossroad Publishing, 1989, 2018), 61.

7.   Richard Rohr interview, *Typology* Season 1, episode 15, October 12, 2017,
https://www.typologypodcast.com/podcast/2017/10/12/richard-rohr
-part2.

8.   Anne Lamott, *Bird by Bird*, 25th Ann. Ed. (New York: Anchor, 2007), 236.

9.   Brené Brown, *The Gifts of Imperfection: Let Go of Who You Think You're
Supposed to Be and Embrace Who You Are* (Center City, MN: Hazelden
Publishing, 2010).

10. Elizabeth Gilbert, *Big Magic: Creative Living Beyond Fear* (New York:
Riverhead Books, 2016), 26.

Chapter 6: The Two's Story

1.   Al Andrews interview, *Typology* Season 3, episode 16, November 14, 2019,
https://www.typologypodcast.com/podcast/2019/14/11/episode03-016/
alandrews.

2.   Beatrice Chestnut interview, *Typology* Season 2, episode 41, May 9, 2019,
https://typology.libsyn.com/bonus-replay-beatrice-chestnut-s02-041.

3.   Lisa-Jo Baker, *Typology* Season 3, episode 25, January 16, 2020, https://www
.typologypodcast.com/podcast/2020/16/01/episode03-025/lisa-jo-baker.

4.   Alice Fryling, *Mirror for the Soul: A Christian Guide to the Enneagram*
(Downers Grove, IL: InterVarsity Press, 2017), 58.

Chapter 7: The Three's Story

1.   Lisa Whelchel interview, *Typology* Season 1, episode 20, November 16,
2017, https://typology.libsyn.com/episode-20-becoming-lisa-welchel. The
excerpt has been edited slightly for readability.

2.   "Lisa Whelchel Reminisces About Her Mickey Mouse Club Days," April
28, 2019, https://www.youtube.com/watch?v=MqGURrCRqBk.

3. Jeff Goins interview, *Typology* Season 1, episode 8, August 24, 2017, https://www.typologypodcast.com/podcast/2017/08/24/episode8/jeffgoins.

4. Don Richard Riso and Russ Hudson, *The Wisdom of the Enneagram: The Complete Guide to Psychological and Spiritual Growth for the Nine Personality Types* (New York: Bantam Books, 1999), 163.

5. Gail Saltz, *Becoming Real: Defeating the Stories We Tell Ourselves That Hold Us Back* (New York: Riverhead Books, 2004), 167.

Chapter 8: The Four's Story

1. Ryan Stevenson interview, *Typology* Season 3, episode 3, August 19, 2019, https://www.typologypodcast.com/podcast/episode03-003/ryanstevenson bestof.

2. Tori Kelly and Andre Murillo interview, *Typology* Season 3, episode 49, July 2, 2020, https://www.typologypodcast.com/podcast/2020/02/07/episode04-001/toriandandre.

3. Russell Moore interview, *Typology* Season 3, episode 39, April 23, 2020, https://www.typologypodcast.com/podcast/2020/23/04/episode03-039/russellmoore.

4. Tsh Oxenreider interview, *Typology* Season 1, episode 4, July 27, 2017, https://typology.libsyn.com/episode-4-tsh-oxenreider-the-art-and-angst-of-living-an-unconventional-life.

5. Ashley Cleveland interview, *Typology* Season 1, episode 48, June 15, 2018, https://www.typologypodcast.com/podcast/2018/13/06/episode47/ashley cleveland.

6. This paragraph is drawn from *Typology* Season 1, episode 39, "May the Fours Be With You," April 12, 2018, https://www.typologypodcast.com/podcast/2018/05/04/episode39/part1fours.

7. Andrew Peterson interview, *Typology* Season 3, episode 15, November 7, 2019, https://www.typologypodcast.com/podcast/2019/07/11/episode3-015/andrewpeterson.

Chapter 9: The Five's Story

1. Kenny Benge interview, *The Road Back to You* podcast Season 1, episode 31, May 3, 2017, https://podcasts.apple.com/us/podcast/gift-thinking-kenny-benge-enneagram-5-investigator/id1130747626?i=1000385082807.

2. Kenny Benge interview, *Typology* Season 1, episode 17, October 26, 2017, https://www.typologypodcast.com/podcast/2017/10/26/episode17/panelof5s.

3. Lori Chaffer interview, *Typology* Season 1, episode 17, October 26, 2017, https://www.typologypodcast.com/podcast/2017/10/26/episode17/panel of5s.

4. Kenny Benge interview, *Typology* Season 1, episode 17, October 26, 2017, https://www.typologypodcast.com/podcast/2017/10/26/episode17/panel of5s.

5. Don Richard Riso and Russ Hudson, *The Wisdom of the Enneagram: The Complete Guide to Psychological and Spiritual Growth for the Nine Personality Types* (New York: Bantam Books, 1999), 217.

6. Andy Root interview, *Typology* Season 1, episode 19, November 9, 2017, https://typology.libsyn.com/episode-19-andy-root.

7. James Joyce, "A Painful Case," in *James Joyce: A Critical Guide*, edited by Lee Spinks (Edinburgh, UK: Edinburgh University Press, 2009), c.

8. Joel Miller interview, *Typology* Season 1, episode 17, October 26, 2017, https://www.typologypodcast.com/podcast/2017/10/26/episode17/panel of5s.

9. Dan Haseltine, *Typology* Season 2, episode 38, April 18, 2019, https://www.typologypodcast.com/podcast/2019/17/04/episodes02-038/danhaseltine.

10. Tim Mackie and Jon Collins interview, *Typology* Season 2, episode 5, August 30, 2018, https://www.typologypodcast.com/podcast/2018/08/30/episode-s02-005/thebibleproject.

11. Helen Palmer, *The Enneagram: Understanding Yourself and the Others in Your Life* (San Francisco: HarperOne, 1988), 231.

Chapter 10: The Six's Story

1. Jill Phillips interview, *Typology* Season 1, episode 10, September 7, 2017, https://www.typologypodcast.com/podcast/2017/09/07/episode10/panel of6s.

2. John Mulaney, audio of "Street Smarts," https://www.youtube.com/watch?v=bXfUsXM01UE.

3. Sarah Thebarge interview, *Typology* Season 1, episode 35, March 15, 2018, https://www.typologypodcast.com/podcast/2018/15/03/episode35/sarahthebarge.

4. Bessel van der Kolk, *The Body Keeps the Score: Brain, Mind, and Body in the Healing of Trauma* (New York: Penguin Books, 2014).

5. Francie Likis interview, *Typology* Season 1, episode 10, September 7, 2017, https://www.typologypodcast.com/podcast/2017/09/07/episode10/panel of6s.

6. Jill Phillips interview, *Typology* Season 3, episode 30, February 20, 2020, https://www.typologypodcast.com/podcast/2020/06/episode-/jillphillips.

7. Leslie Jordan interview, *Typology* Season 1, episode 10, September 7, 2017, https://www.typologypodcast.com/podcast/2017/09/07/episode10/panelof6s.

Chapter 11: The Seven's Story

1. Shauna and Aaron Niequist, *Typology* Season 1, episode 13, September 28, 2017, https://www.typologypodcast.com/podcast/2017/09/28/episode13/shaunaaaronniequist.

2. See Rob Bell interview, Premier TV, July 22, 2008, https://www.youtube.com/watch?v=5KujG5Ww1bQ. You can also purchase his audio book *Blood, Guts, and Fire: The Gospel According to Leviticus* at https://gumroad.com/l/blood-guts-fire.

3. Rob Bell interview, *Typology* Season 1, episode 1, July 6, 2017, https://typology.libsyn.com/01-rob-bell-an-enneagram-7-with-a-7-wing.

4. Bob and Maria Goff interview, *Typology* Season 1, episode 2, July 13, 2017, https://typology.libsyn.com/episode-2-bob-maria-goff-the-beautifully-imperfect-marriage-of-a-9-7.

5. This saying is popularly attributed to Carl Jung, but it is likely a paraphrase and accurate documentation is elusive.

6. Alice Fryling, *Mirror for the Soul: A Christian Guide to the Enneagram* (Downers Grove, IL: InterVarsity Press, 2017), 80.

Chapter 12: The Larger Story

1. Quoted in Ann Trieger Kurland in the *Boston Globe* online, https://bostonglobe.com/2020/11/17/lifestyle/fans-adore-quoting-julia-child-often-get-it-wrong-this-book-can-help/, updated November 17, 2020.

2. Frederick Buechner, "Grace," in *Beyond Words* (San Francisco: HarperOne, 2004), 139.

3. Maya Angelou, interview by Oprah Winfrey, Super Soul Sunday, OWN, Ep. 416, May 19, 2013.

4. Attributed to eighteenth-century Polish rabbi Baal Shem Tov, founder of the Jewish spiritual movement known as Hasidism.

About the Author

Ian Morgan Cron is a bestselling author, psychotherapist, expert Enneagram teacher, Episcopal priest, Dove Award–winning songwriter, and the host of the popular podcast *Typology*. His books include the novel *Chasing Francis*; the spiritual memoir *Jesus, My Father, the CIA, and Me*; and *The Road Back to You: An Enneagram Journey to Self-Discovery*.

Known for his transparency, humor, and insight into the inner workings of the human heart and mind, Ian uses the Enneagram personality-typing system as a tool to help people cultivate self-awareness and emotional wisdom. He is a highly sought after speaker for large conferences and corporate boardrooms alike. He and his wife, Anne, have three children and live in Nashville, Tennessee.

To start your Enneagram journey, read Ian's book *The Road Back to You* and take Ian's free Enneagram typing assessment (please visit www.ianmorgancron.com).

To discover more about how to become the highest expression of yourself, please visit www.typologyinstitute.com.

For more about Ian, including information on speaking engagements, the *Typology* podcast, and interview requests, please visit www.ianmorgancron.